American Insider's Guide to

Twentieth-century Furniture

John Sollo
Nan Sollo

General Editor: Lita Solis-Cohen

Eugene Schoen's furniture and accessories, designed and made during the 1930s,
are much admired today for their refined elegance, warmth, and subtle use of color.

American Insider's Guide to
Twentieth-century
Furniture

To those who saw it first: Barry, Mark, Ralph, Mark, Alan, Tony, Linda, Don, Curt, Jacques, Michael, Frank, Chris, Rando, Sandy, Otis, Martha, Billy, Rick, Nick, Ken, to name just a few. And to our beautiful daughter, Megan, whose college tuition ate up every dime we earned from this book (spending money not included!).

American Insider's Guide to Twentieth-century Furniture

A Miller's-Mitchell Beazley book
Published by Octopus Publishing Group Ltd.
2–4 Heron Quays
London E14 4JP
U.K.

Commissioning Editor: Anna Sanderson
Executive Art Editor: Rhonda Fisher
U.S. Project Manager: Joseph Gonzalez

Produced by:
designsection
Caxton Road
Frome
Somerset BA11 1DY
U.K.

General Editor: Lita Solis-Cohen
Editor: Julian Flanders
Graphic Design: Carole McDonald
Proofreader: Carol Mauro-Noon
Indexer: Indexing Specialists

ISBN 1 84000 379 0

Set in Perpetua.
Printed and bound in Hong Kong.

Miller's is a registered trademark of Octopus Publishing Group Ltd.

Front cover picture: Storage Unit (ESU) Series, *c.* 1952, Charles & Ray Eames
Back cover picture: Child's chair and stool, *c.* 1945, Charles & Ray Eames
Back flap picture: Flag Halyard Chair *c.* 1949 by Hans Wegner

CONTENTS

INTRODUCTION

The story of Modernism is the story of change. It is the triumph of possibility and imagination over the oppression of an entrenched status quo. Modernism is a manifestation of humankind's belief and hope for the future. It is about our willingness to look forward with a sense of adventure and optimism, unhindered by the constrictions of the past. It is the unshackling of the human spirit to pursue artistic vision in ways not yet thought of, unexplored and unsanctioned. At its most fundamental level, Modernism is the story of revolution, of anarchy eclipsing control and the creative power of chaos—a celebration of individual expression.

Twentieth-century design is a schizophrenic jungle of competing thoughts, theories and absolutes. Modernism is simultaneously progressive and conservative, socially conscious and profit oriented. It relies on ornamentation and worships minimalism, is excessive and functional, handcrafted and machine made, employs natural materials and space-age synthetics; can be represented by both international corporations and a guy in his studio. Modern is early, late, big, small, French, German, postwar, prewar, streamlined, Scandinavian, American and Japanese. Like the 20th century itself, Modern design is a morass of contradictions and conflicts.

The pursuit of Modern introduces collectors to a world of possibility. They can choose to collect the luxurious excess of French Art Deco or the extreme minimalism and functionalism of Bauhaus production. Enthusiasts can pursue American streamlined, Scandinavian organic or Italian post-Modern and still refer to themselves as Modern collectors. Nor is Modern collecting relegated only to furniture. Lighting, dinnerware, rugs, art, architectural elements, vacuum cleaners and even

More comfortable than it looks, this Jan chair typifies Modern furniture's irreverence toward tradition and convention. $1,000–$2,000

toasters are all heavily influenced by the many phases of Modernism, and all are eagerly sought after by collectors.

The collecting of Modern is still in an early stage. There is youthful exuberance and passion—a sense of adventure and discovery surrounding the collecting of 20th-century design. Great finds are still out there and an air of possibility abounds. Great examples of 20th-century genius are still reasonably priced and good things are inexpensive.

Few other areas of collecting offer the average person such an opportunity to touch the past. There are literally hundreds of 20th-century masters waiting to be discovered. Their work is hidden in garages and basements, forgotten by time and history. Twentieth-century design provides the opportunity to engage in urban archaeology to a degree unmatched by other fields of collecting interest.

The bent-plywood stool by Sori Yanagi is a remarkable Modern form.
$600–$900

Mies Van der Rohe for Knoll. This rare bronze Barcelona chair and ottoman realized $5,000 at auction. The more common chrome-plated steel version generally brings $1,500 to $2,000 at auction.

BUYING AND SELLING

In the beginning, collecting Modernist furniture was a pursuit limited to the urban corridors of America, largely the domain of art teachers, architects and the aesthetically courageous. Today, opportunities abound for collectors to purchase Modern decorative arts and furniture. Enthusiasts in almost all geographic areas have access to a wide range of Modern material, unprecedented even 10 years ago.

As interest in Modern has moved into the mainstream, demand for mid-century design has grown exponentially along with the dealers, brokers and auctioneers willing to meet that demand.

Interestingly, prices still remain regionalized, with furniture prices varying from city to city and state to state. Los Angeles enthusiasts tend to prefer indigenous designers like Schindler, Neutra and Bertram Sherman, while New Yorkers gravitate toward designers of High Style furniture—Samuel Marx, Tommy Parzinger and Edward Wormley. These trends can change seemingly overnight, sometimes with a new exhibition at an important urban museum or even a current issue of a popular design magazine.

Another notable trend in the world of Modern is the tremendous growth of interest in 20th century accent pieces. Owners of homes filled with Dunbar sofas and Nakashima dining-room sets have turned their collecting energy toward lighting, rugs, clocks and Modern art and sculpture. This can be seen in record auction prices for such items as Angelo Testa rugs, Howard Miller clocks and Arteluce lighting.

Modern is still in a dynamic state. Unlike other collecting venues, Modern has been enthusiastically accepting of work done by both major and minor contributors. The discovery of new designers is an ongoing process, adding depth, texture and uncertainty to the market. Unlike traditional areas of collecting, Modern covers large geographic areas and a long time span. From the turn-of-the-century Secessionists to Postmodernists like Wendell Castle and Gaetano Pesce, Modern design encompasses the whole of the 20th century. It also crosses many national boundaries. Modernism's contributors are an international cast ranging from the Bauhaus of Germany and French Art Deco to Scandinavian organic Modernism and American pre- and postwar industrial designs. This leaves the collector with a myriad of opportunities to acquire unique, exciting material.

One of the most exciting aspects of collecting Modern is the possibility it offers of purchasing the very best examples: one-of-a-kind and museum-quality pieces, at reasonable prices. Not since the early years of the last century when Wallace Nutting

This sculpture-front sideboard by Paul Evans challenges conventional furniture boundaries and illustrates the creative extremes favored by Modern furniture designers.
$8,000–$12,000

and other pioneer collectors of Colonial American antiques canvassed the countryside has the opportunity presented itself to buy the very best of a period for reasonable prices.

Nowadays, Chippendale and Tiffany objects are limited to a few exclusive auction houses and dealers and collectors with deep pockets but the average person can still afford to put together a world-class collection of Modern design. The treasure hunt is still on, and great finds can be made anywhere from dusty antique shops and flea markets to thrift shops and small, local auction houses and estate sales. This is what keeps Modernism vibrant and fresh and helps to attract new enthusiasts to this young and ever-expanding market.

The use of new and radical materials has always been an important feature of Modern design. Plastic was particularly popular during the pop movement of the 1960s.
$600–$900

BUYING AND SELLING AT AUCTION

Attending a live auction can be an exciting, informative affair. Auction houses provide the collector with an insider's view of both quantities of quality material and insights into the vagaries of the fickle Modern market. This provides a perfect vantage point to watch design history being made.

At auction, Modern enthusiasts have the opportunity to view, touch and examine a diverse range of 20th-century icons. This hands-on experience can significantly elevate any collector's knowledge base.

If you are attending an auction in person, it is very important to examine items of interest. Even after a close examination it is helpful to ask auction personnel about provenance, repair and refinishing that may not be readily discernible. If you are interested in a lot and cannot preview the item in person, make sure to request a detailed condition report. The report should contain information about provenance, repair, restoration and dimensions. Ask for photos of the entire piece and close-ups of details. Many auctioneers post photos on their web sites.

A few minutes spent reading the terms and conditions of sales for a particular auction house can save the buyer a good deal of grief. Special attention should be given to the guarantee section, oftentimes referred to as warranties. There is no common standard for auction-house guarantees. Some houses sell all things "as is—where is," offering the buyer no recourse; other houses offer limited guarantees that provide the purchaser with some protection against questionable authenticity. A few auction houses have unconditional guarantees, but these are rare.

In today's competitive market most auction houses charge a buyer's premium. This is a commission on your purchase that is a percentage of the hammer price. These fees range between 5 and 20 percent.

Modern furniture designers often developed pieces with a strong sculptural presence. This Verner Panton Heart chair from the mid-1960s is a good example.
$6,000–$9,000.

Make sure to calculate this figure into the highest price you are willing to pay for an item so there are no surprises at the check-out desk.

It is also good to know the methods of billing and shipping. Most auctions will arrange with private companies to ship purchases but the costs vary widely.

Many auction houses allow consignors to protect their property with a reserve. A reserve is simply the price below which an auction house will not sell an item. Auctioneers cannot reveal specific dollar amounts of the reserves. A lot with a reserve placed on it should be so marked in the catalog. Most auction houses do not allow reserves to exceed the low estimate. In some cities this is law, but more often it is a stated policy of individual auctions.

Auction catalogs can provide a source of invaluable information for the collector. Catalogs usually have color photos and detailed descriptions of lots including manufacturers, designers and years

of production. Also very helpful is the auction house custom of providing estimates for lots being sold. This gives collectors a general idea of what similar examples may bring.

Without a doubt, the most productive and enjoyable way to bid at auction is in person. This option allows bidders to watch the action, get a feel for the auctioneer's rhythm, see who the other buyers are and pick up bargains on things that may fall outside the interest of the in-house crowd. Another advantage is the ability to connect with other collectors and dealers with similar interests. If you cannot attend an auction in person, however, several other options exist.

The most popular is phone bidding. Auction houses reserve a phone in your name, and you are called several minutes prior to the time the desired lot comes up. The bidder is included in the live action in house. It is important to call well in advance to arrange a phone bid. In some instances phone bidding is used only on higher priced lots.

A common form of absentee bidding is to leave a bid with the auction house. "Left bids" are the highest price a prospective bidder is willing to pay for a given item. It is vital to know how bids will be executed during the auction. Reputable houses execute a bid just as if the potential buyer were present, and the lot opens at the prearranged opening price. Some houses, however, use the left bid as a starting point in hopes of finding one bid higher. Be sure to ask how your absent bid will be handled.

Live internet bidding at auctions is now an available option. This holds some advantages over phone bidding. With phone bidding you commit to a definite lot, but with live internet bidding you have access to any piece in the auction. The bidding is done in real time. This affords the bidder the opportunity to watch the trends at a specific auction and jump in and bid when there are good buys to be made.

Selling at auction can often be just as exciting as buying. In every auction crowd there are usually a number of sellers present who are eager to share in the excitement of the live crowd. It is also a way to profit from larger, urban markets not always available to many sellers.

In addition, auctions allow the seller to take advantage of the technical expertise and knowledge of the auction staff and national marketing networks. Auctions also shield the seller from the haggling, dickering and time involved in selling items privately. Many sellers wish to retain their anonymity for various reasons and most auctions protect their privacy carefully.

It is an important responsibility of the prospective Modern seller to find an auction house well versed in Modern merchandise. Many houses have very specific specialties and are not particularly knowledgeable about design movements outside their range.

Commission rates vary from auction to auction. Sellers should check to see if there are additional charges for photography, storage and insurance. Auction houses will often pick up items as part of the overall commission structure or for a fee. Discuss your expectations in regard to estimates and reserves.

It is always exciting to see your lots show up in a color catalog that gets sent to clients around the world, and you never know—your piece may set a market record.

INTERNET BUYING AND SELLING

An intriguing option for buying and selling Modern merchandise is the successful addition of internet auctions into mainstream Modern promotion. eBay and a number of other auction sites, including Sothebys.com, offer Modernists access to goods on a worldwide basis. Since eBay's inception, Modern collectibles have been a staple component of its auction inventory. While many of these pieces tend to be more "kitschy," rare museum-quality pieces show up regularly, and there are buyers and sellers from every level of the Modern market looking for items.

Shipping and billing are the responsibility of the internet seller, and there are now guarantors who ensure proper payment procedures for your convenience. The seller also has the ability to set a time frame for the sale and reserves for individual items, which keeps control in the hands of the vendor. Buyers can check on the general reliability of the seller through the site.

Although internet selling doesn't have the same glamor or excitement as regular auction action does, internet auctions are a relatively easy, inexpensive method in which to expose your treasure to a global market. A number of books have been published recently on successful selling techniques, and many auction sites offer helpful information on how to get started.

The internet has become a fertile hunting ground for collectors of Modern furniture.

BUYING FROM DEALERS

Increasing interest in Modernism has created a wellspring of enthusiastic, knowledgeable dealers across the country.

In addition to providing quality mid-century merchandise, dealers provide an important source of information for collectors. Today most urban areas support multiple retail dealers whose goods range from fun and kitschy to museum-quality items.

Purchasing from dealers offers a number of advantages: easy access to material, personal service and links to wider markets as a result of dealer networking. Unlike auctions that are held infrequently and are found only in large urban areas, dealers do the legwork and hauling and usually have an inventory readily available for buyers all the time and in a wide range of locations.

Personal service is advantageous when hunting down esoteric or one-of-a-kind items. A good long-term relationship with a dealer can be invaluable in building major collections. Dealers often have access to private sellers and museum pieces that do not come to auction or mainstream markets. They also often know dealers in markets that differ from their own and have the ability to procure merchandise from these dealers.

Dealers also can be flexible in their pricing, and the better the buying relationship, the better the discounts may be for good customers. Having a network of good dealers is of tremendous benefit to any serious collector.

SELLING TO DEALERS

Selling merchandise to dealers has many advantages. First and foremost is expedience. Unlike auction houses, which hold two Modern sales per year, dealers are always eager for fresh merchandise, and they are always buying. Sales can be accomplished in a very short period of time.

A second plus is convenience. There are dealers all over the country. Many are willing to visit you

Marcel Breuer's first American commission was to design desks, chairs and other furniture for a Bryn Mawr college dormitory.
Desk, $3,000–$4,000
Chairs, $3,000–$5,000 each

Classics like these Eames pieces are easy to find through dealers:

Ten-panel screen, $8,000–$12,000
Rockers, $800–$1,200 each
DCM chairs, $200–$400 each

personally, and most can arrange transportation for items immediately. There is no waiting for payment either. Dealers pay on receipt of merchandise.

Another advantage to the seller is that many dealers are willing to trade, offering the opportunity to upgrade a collection with a minimum cash outlay on the part of the collector. Dealers often buy pieces with specific customers in mind and often have a large network of other dealers and shops with which they do business.

There is often more flexibility in a dealer transaction than in other ways of selling. Developing a good relationship with a reputable dealer can bring with it better terms for the buyer or seller. There are dealers who offer to take merchandise on consignment. It is important to examine the details of any business arrangement, and selling or consigning

to dealers is no exception. Check percentages and find out who will be insuring a consigned item. Do your homework. Know what you are selling and to whom you are selling.

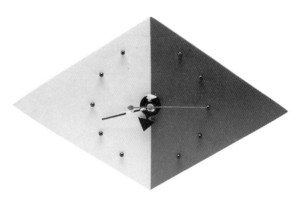

Unique or prototypical examples of Modern design often excite the passions of collectors. This rare Nelson clock brought $14,000 at auction.

This Pedro Frieberg Hand chair is a rare icon of Modern design. $3,000–$4,000.

TRADE SHOWS

As the number of Modern collectors has increased, and the market has matured, many more Modern shopping opportunities have become available for the 20th-century enthusiast. An important development that has helped to expose collectors to large quantities of Modern material has been the advent of the Modern show. Held at venues across the country, Modern shows have become great places to view quality material and ask specific questions of dealers. One interesting aspect of shows is the geographic diversity represented. Usually dealers from across

North America and oftentimes Europe, will participate, offering the collector the potential to view regionally specific merchandise.

Other advantages of attending shows are of an educational nature. Almost all major shows offer lectures and slide presentations on various areas of Modernism. Also many dealers save their most rare, interesting or challenging pieces for display at shows. Dealers may also be motivated to negotiate prices, especially before the closing of the show. Another advantage of attending a Modern show can be the opportunity to view merchandise that dealers without retail space would be unable to show. Often these dealers will use a particular show as their sole sales venue.

FLEA MARKETS

A major factor in America's love affair with antiques and collectibles is the ubiquitous outdoor flea market. Scattered across America, flea markets offer easy access to a wide range of merchandise, both good and bad.

Outdoor flea markets have been popular with collectors since the 1950s. Utilizing parking lots, drive-in movie theaters, cow pastures and large sports stadiums, these shows offer shoppers an opportunity to increase their collections, sometimes at bargain prices.

There are, however, several important caveats for flea market shoppers. First is that, like time, good Modern at bargain prices waits for no one. Get there early and move fast. The successful flea market shopper is up before dawn and must be quick, efficient and aggressive. The best buys are often made by approaching dealers who are just setting up for the day.

Many successful shoppers ask dealers what they have, or recite a mantra-like list of what they are

Flea markets can be good fun, good exercise and good places to find Modern furniture at the right price.

looking for. The first hour of any successful flea market adventure should be spent covering as much ground and investigating as many booths as possible. Bargains do not sit around waiting for you to stumble upon them.

When intriguing merchandise is found, it is critical to examine it carefully for condition, age and authenticity. Some flea market dealers purchase portions of their inventory at garage and estate sales on Fridays, load this merchandise into their vehicles and sell it at flea markets on Saturdays or Sundays. This short turnover time does not allow for lengthy examination of a piece or any kind of professional restoration.

This "quick flip" can be advantageous from a collector's perspective as it does not allow the seller time to research the value of a piece, opening up the possibility of acquiring a great piece at a bargain price. An advantage unique to the Modernist market is that many flea market dealers, while very knowledgeable about general antiques, may not be

versed in the fine points of 20th-century design, opening up the possibility of a good buy.

Another point to remember when shopping an outdoor market is to be environmentally prepared. Bring a raincoat, water, snacks, hat and suntan lotion. Comfortable shoes are a must. Great shoppers bring small bills with them so valuable time won't be lost fumbling to make change. Experienced flea marketers haggle only when necessary for a great piece but otherwise don't waste time trying to get an extra 10 percent taken off the price.

There are outdoor flea markets and antique shows that have become legendary in today's antiques business: Brimfield, Kane County, 26th Street and Sixth Avenue in New York City and the Rose Bowl, just to name a few. To many dealers and collectors, going to these events takes on the overtones of a religious pilgrimage; work, weddings and vacations are all planned around important flea market weekends.

Modern classics, like this Bertoia chair, can be found at flea markets, but it helps to get there early.

STARTING A COLLECTION

At no point during the life of collecting is there more excitement and enthusiasm than at the beginning of the process. There are new concepts to be understood, new people to meet, great and beautiful objects to be purchased. There are also many pitfalls that can blur and complicate collecting. Taking a few simple precautions can minimize most of these.

First, learn as much as possible before starting to spend the mortgage money on merchandise. With the mainstreaming of Modern, there are numerous books and magazines that can be used to glean important information. In many urban centers there are Modern shows that offer the collector the opportunity to talk with knowledgeable dealers from around the world and to view and evaluate large and diverse displays of available merchandise. There are also Modern shops and galleries across America that can provide would-be collectors with helpful information. Knowledge is power when it comes to building a collection.

A fundamental mistake made by many collectors is not focusing on a specific area of collecting interest. The Modern movement covers the entire 20th century and includes lamps, sculpture, art, glassware, furniture, ceramics, silver and textiles, architectural elements and even books and posters—pretty much anything produced by the human hand. That is a big arena for collecting. Successful collectors constantly redefine their interests and refine their particular goals and focus.

Another common mistake is to begin collections with mediocre or mundane examples. There is quite a bit of Modern material to be had in the marketplace. Buy the best examples in the best condition available to you at the time. Shop and compare before purchasing a piece. It is also a good idea to take advantage of the opportunities to trade up—selling or trading a lesser example in order to obtain a more important or desirable one.

These chairs were designed by Florence Knoll for office and residential use.
$600–$900 the pair

Collecting Modern furniture offers wonderful opportunities to people in any and every income bracket. People can collect the work of George Nakashima or Wharton Esherick and spend hundreds of thousands of dollars in the process, or they can collect Machine-age household items and spend hundreds of dollars. These extremes in the valuation of Modern material are an important part of its continuing and growing popularity.

Finally, have fun. Collecting should be a passion, not a punishment. Enjoy learning and sharing your knowledge with the people you encounter along the way. Happy hunting!

This Laurel lamp is a good example of less expensive Modern lighting.
$400–$600

PROTOTYPES VS. PRODUCTION MODELS

One of the most exciting aspects to collecting Modern furniture is the possibility of finding and acquiring unique prototypes, like the "Joe" chair, shown below.

Many designers or their employees carted prototypes home, storing them in their garages or basements. Discovering these historically significant examples can lead to new insights into the evolution of Modernism. Because of their rarity, prototypes often bring much higher prices than production models.

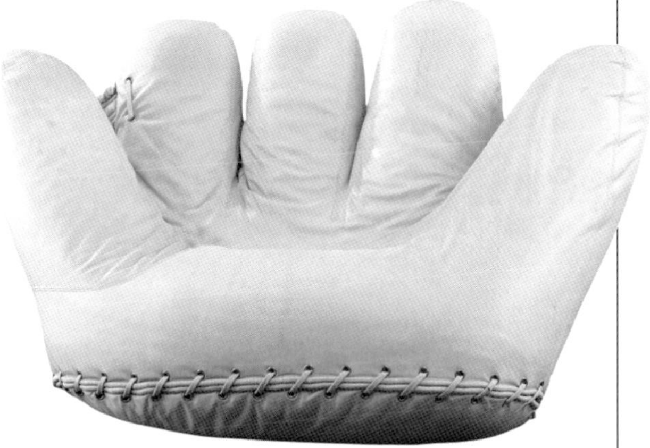

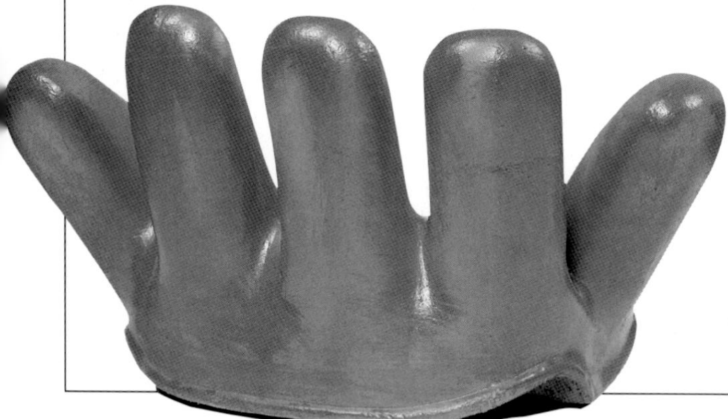

Left: "Joe" chair prototype, c. 1969. Manufactured by Jonathon DePas, Donato d'Urbino & Paolo Lomazzi.
$8,000–$12,000
Above: The "Joe" Baseball Glove chair by Pas d'Urbino & Lamazzi for Poltronova / Stendig.
$3,000–$4,000

CARE AND REPAIR

UPHOLSTERED PIECES

Although many case goods have made the trip through the 20th century relatively unscathed, upholstered furniture is usually not as fortunate.

Upholstered furniture usually gets the bulk of use in homes and commercial interiors, so the chance of finding any Modern upholstered pieces in mint condition is low.

The good news is that reupholstering can often enhance the value of fine custom furniture. It is important to assess the value of a finished piece to make sure that the investment in new upholstery can be absorbed by the value of the piece. For example, a George Nelson Coconut chair whose upholstery is in poor condition can take up to $2,000 to return to near original condition, but may bring as much as $8,000 with its ottoman. However, the cost of reupholstering more modest or common pieces like a Frank Lloyd Wright sofa for Henredon or a 1950s Paul McCobb chair by Directional cannot be offset by their retail value on today's secondary market.

Modern upholstery often takes unusual forms. There are biomorphic shapes, angles and curves that present problems for the average upholsterer. Foam pieces have their own difficulties. Verner Panton Heart chairs and even Knoll Diamond and Bird chairs tend to dry out in arid climates. Stendig's Marilyn sofa, Pesce's Five Up chair and several other foam pieces often need extensive restoration and expert attention to return them to near original condition. This work demands a high level of expertise to retain the value of the item. It is important to find the right upholsterer for the job. Poor reupholstery can make a piece less valuable than one with original upholstery in poor condition.

Upholstery in poor condition does not affect the price of these Nakashima pieces. Collectors generally don't mind replacing the fabric on a nice example of Nakashima furniture, and reupholstering does little to devalue it.

Leather upholstery can be very expensive to replace. If pieces are still in production it is often helpful to contact the manufacturer and inquire about replacement fabrics.

Eames compact sofas, unlike some Modern forms, are easy to refoam and recover.

In sculptural pieces, like Stendig's Marilyn sofa, it's important to pay attention to the condition of the foam. Replacing it can be a daunting challenge.

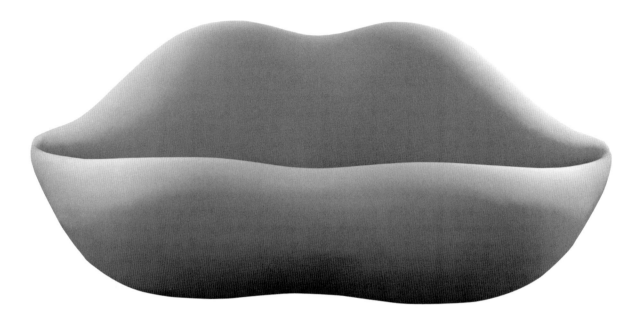

Many of the fabrics used in the last half of the 20th century were synthetic and stained easily. In the last twenty or so years, stain-removal technologies have been greatly improved and new chemical treatments can often remove stains thought permanent only a few years ago. The collector can sometimes avoid the cost of reupholstering by removing stains or having them removed by professionals.

Upholstered furniture also absorbs odors easily and may smell smoky or musty from years in storage. There are several fairly effective treatments available to rid pieces of their odors. Good upholstery cleaning services can usually help with this.

Covers for Bird and Diamond chairs can still be special ordered through Knoll in a wide selection of fabrics very similar to the original covers. Several other companies also manufacture "retro" type fabrics, and synthetics used on various pieces and even original fabrics show up in the marketplace and at auction on a regular basis.

It is important to purchase leather-covered Modern seating in the best condition possible. A seemingly good buy can lure people into buying leather pieces in poor condition at a sale or auction, but it is usually very expensive to redo most leather furniture. Herman Miller is still selling replacement leather pads for its Eames lounge chairs, but reupholstering a leather Mies Barcelona chair with its intricate tufting and welting is usually a significant investment.

Some leather can be reconditioned with neetsfoot or other oils, but avoid leather that is cracked. Hot and dry climates also dry out leather so it may be helpful to examine leather pieces carefully for splitting or brittleness. Dried-out leather usually cannot be restitched successfully.

Paying a premium price for upholstered Modern furniture in great condition may seem exhorbitant, but it may actually be less expensive than having the piece recovered, especially if you factor in the time and effort required to find the right craftsperson for the job.

RESTORING CASE GOODS

At this point in the history of collecting Modern, there is debate about refinishing. While it is generally preferred that pieces be in good original condition, refinished pieces are often accepted just as eagerly in the marketplace as items that have not been restored. This may come as a surprise to those who collect furniture from other eras. A large part of the value of period furniture, for example, hinges on its remaining in original paints or finishes—even when the original finish may be chipped, cracked or faded. With Modern, repair work or refinishing may be preferable to finish damage.

Modern enthusiasts seem to accept that most of this furniture was used daily and may need work to bring it back to near original condition. Many people live with their Modern collection as part of their home furnishings and prefer that damage be repaired.

The designers and manufacturers of Modern furniture were highly innovative in their use of materials and joining systems, and their experimental techniques were "cutting edge" in their time. Restorers of Modern furniture need to be flexible and creative. They must deal with everything from the simple oil finishes on George Nakashima furniture to the thin veneer on George Nelson pieces and the colored lacquer used on many Modern pieces, as well as splits and breaks in

Knoll still supplies replacement covers for Bertoia side chairs (left), Bird chairs (center), and Diamond chairs (right). Check the welds on the metal frames of Bertoia chairs as they often break and are difficult to weld cleanly back into place.

For parts in good enough condition, fiberglass and plastic cleaning products are usually available at boat dealers. To a limited extent these can help improve finishes that suffer from certain condition problems. Many dealers have taken fiberglass pieces to companies that do bodywork on boats or Corvettes with varying degrees of success.

Plastic and fiberglass furniture with serious structural problems can often seem like a bargain but much of it is not repairable and has little or no value for serious collectors.

METAL

Metal is an integral part of much of 20th-century high-style design. Metal technologies have made tremendous advances during the era of Modernism. Today's metals are lighter and stronger, and fastening and plating technologies have improved.

Collectors often find metal pieces that have broken welds, rust or dents and breaks. As with all restoration, be sure to ascertain the finished value before proceeding with any major work.

Rechroming can be extremely expensive and is not often available outside larger metropolitan areas. Welding is difficult on lower-quality metal, and cracks or breaks make metal furniture structurally unsound. Look carefully at undersides and areas hidden from normal view for weaknesses. Many a collector has gotten a piece of furniture home only to discover that, in their excitement to find something good, they didn't spend enough time carefully inspecting the merchandise.

Some metal furniture has parts that can be replaced. Herman Miller still does repair work on much of its furniture. Hardware is also available for a large percentage of its lines. Other companies no longer carry discontinued parts or are no longer in business. Many dealers have access to parts because they have purchased pieces in poor condition specifically for their useable parts. Spend some time researching availability. The closer a piece comes to its original condition, the higher its value. It's worth the investment in time looking for pieces in as close to original condition as possible.

The seats and backs of Eames chairs, like those shown here, can separate from the legs if the rubber shock mounts dry out. Many Eames parts are still available from the Herman Miller Company which will also repair these problems for a reasonable fee.

DISPLAYING MODERN FURNITURE

Open the pages of any American or international design magazine and you will inevitably see a wonderful piece of Modern furniture comfortably ensconced amid folk art, period pieces, contemporary and even European antiques. From stark, cool Modernist architecture to country manses, Modern seems able to make a niche for itself.

Displaying Modern objects is actually easy. Many collectors are purists who prefer one major style to another; others are able to see the connections and interplay among the different styles when placed side by side in the same interior. Many pieces of studio furniture, such as the work of George Nakashima or Wharton Esherick, are exotic stand-alones, but most fine Modern objects have such classic forms that they can blend comfortably in almost any setting. Most are practical, well made and intended for normal use, and do not require any special attention.

As with any collector's objects the more rare and fragile pieces should be displayed away from the main traffic areas of the home. Finer ceramics and pottery are better off shelved for safety's sake, but very few Modern items need special attention. With regular care and maintenance Modern can and ought to be enjoyed in day-to-day living and should hold up for a long time.

Decorating with Modern furniture is often a lot like decorating with sculptural art. Successfully integrating a high-impact piece, like this Frank Gehry Bubbles chaise longue, in an interior takes planning, forethought and a good eye.

STYLES OF MODERN FURNITURE

There were many design movements during the span of the 20th century, making Modernism seem like a chaotic blend of competing styles and disciplines. But all the styles were based on reform, a reaction to the excesses of the Victorian age. They offer something new, simple and functional. "Truth to materials," "a machine for living," "form follows function" are 20th-century mantras. In each decade, it seems, a new style was championed by a small group of avant-garde tastemakers. Today, collectors embrace all the styles, scholars have documented them, museums exhibit them and dealers and auctioneers search for and find the best examples they can muster for the marketplace.

PARLOR SUITE BY JOSEF HOFFMANN,
c. 1905
$3,000–$4,000

WORMLEY FOR DUNBAR COFFEE TABLE WITH NATZLER TILE INSERTS, c. 1958
$4,000–$6,000

ETTORE SOTTSASS CARLTON BOOKCASE,
c. 1981
$12,000–$18,000

FRANK LLOYD WRIGHT CHAIR,
c. 1952
$8,000–$12,000

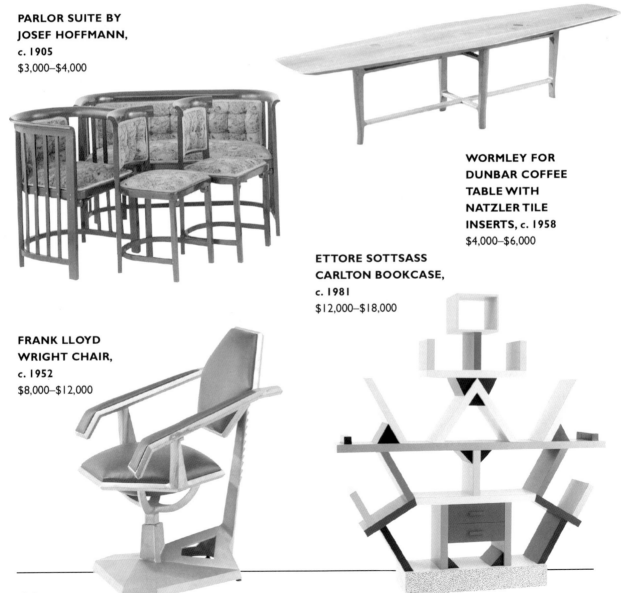

Arts and Crafts 1880–1915

William Morris and John Ruskin, two Englishmen who promoted the idea of handcraftsmanship and saw the industrialization of art and design as dehumanizing, were major forces behind the Arts and Crafts Movement. They turned to a romanticized vision of Medieval Europe for design reference, and produced furniture that was without excessive ornamentation. In America, the furniture and decorative objects of Gustav Stickley and the Roycrofters were leading exponents of the Arts and Crafts style.

The Arts and Crafts market is considerably older and more established than the Modern market. Prices are higher, and important examples can be much more difficult to find. The Arts and Crafts market also places a great deal of importance on pieces that are in pristine original condition.

GUSTAV STICKLEY DROP FRONT DESK, c. 1902
This rare and early fall-front desk typifies the work of Arts and Crafts master Gustav Stickley.
$80,000–$120,000

GUSTAV STICKLEY SIDEBOARD, c.1905
This Stickley sideboard shows the design influences of Harvey Ellis.
$40,000–$50,000

Weiner Werkestätte 1903–1933

Led by Josef Hoffmann and Koloman Moser, the Weiner Werkestätte was a Viennese reform movement committed to eliminating historical and naturalistic motifs in design. Heavily influenced by Glasgow architect Rennie Mackintosh, Hoffmann and his fellow "secessionists," as they were called, relied on the power of geometric and rectilinear forms to provide an element of ornamentation. Like those in the Arts and Crafts Movement, the secessionists were wary of the effect of industrialization and the machine on art and design. Instead, they chose to emphasize the role of handcraftsmanship in their work. The secessionists produced a wide array of furniture, graphics, ceramics, glassware, textiles and metalwork.

Furniture designed by secessionist masters is eagerly sought after by collectors. Though rare in America, secessionist pieces do come to the marketplace every so often.

SECESSIONIST CABINET, c. 1910
A burl wood cabinet in the manner of Josef Hoffmann.
$2,000–$3,000

OTTO WAGNER CHAIRS, c. 1905
These sleek chairs were designed by secessionist architect Otto Wagner for his Vienna Post Office Savings Bank building.
$2,000–$3,000 the pair

JOSEF HOFFMANN CHAIR, c. 1905
A Hoffmann classic, this chair was designed for the Purkensdorf sanitarium and produced by J. & J. Kohn.
$2,000–$3,000

Bauhaus 1919–1933

The Bauhaus was one of the most important influences on Modern design in the 20th Century. Organized by Walter Gropius in Weimar, Germany, the Bauhaus had as either students or faculty some of the most innovative and creative members of the 20th-century design community. They developed one of the most defining and fundamental principles of Modernist theory: the idea that form should follow function. The Bauhaus also promoted the notion that mass production and craft were compatible, and supported a symbiotic relationship between art and industry.

Today, furniture designs from the Bauhaus look simple and unextraordinary, but when they were first introduced, these pieces were considered extremely radical and shocked the design world. Bauhaus designs remain enormously influential, and very collectible, to this day. Early examples bring a premium.

MIES van der ROHE ARMCHAIR, c. 1930
Van der Rohe's cantilevered armchair, below, was produced by the Thonet Company.
$5,000–$7,000

MIES van der ROHE MR10 CHAIR, c. 1927
Another cantilevered design by Mies van der Rohe, the M.R. chair, below, is still popular with designers 75 years after its original production.
$3,000–$4,000

MARCEL BREUER ARMCHAIR, c. 1930
Designed by Marcel Breuer for the Metz Company of Amsterdam, this rare chair is a classic example of form following function.
$5,000–$7,000

MIES van der ROHE DAY BED, c. 1970
Many Bauhaus designs are still in production today. This van der Rohe day bed is produced by the Knoll Company
$4,000–$6,000 for this Knoll production

Art Deco 1920–1940

In direct contrast with the functionalism of the Bauhaus, Art Deco celebrated opulence and glamor. Art Deco relied on a diverse array of distinctive ornamental devices to imbue an object with a sense of luxury. The Art Deco style drew upon many different inspirations, including nature, geometric patterns, and jazz themes. Its vocabulary was applied to a wide range of objects and greatly influenced the architecture of the period.

Some of the 20th-century's most beautiful, elaborate and luxurious furniture was created in the Art Deco style. A truly international phenomenon, Art Deco was the design language of Frenchmen Jean Michel Frank, Jacques Ruhlman and Edgar Brandt, as well as Americans Paul Frankl and Donald Deskey. Art Deco's indulgence of aesthetic passions makes it very popular with collectors.

DONALD DESKEY DRESSERS, c. 1935
Art Deco dressers by one of America's premier Modern designers.
$3,000–$4,000 each

EDGAR BRANDT CEILING LAMP, c.1925

The opulence and grandeur of the Art Deco style is evident in this tiered ceiling lamp by the French Art Deco designer Edgar Brandt with a Daum etched-glass shade.

$15,000–$20,000

DECO TABLE, c.1935

Art Deco abstract designs decorate the base and legs of this outstanding round table.

$2,000–$3,000

ROHDE PALDAO SIDEBOARD, c.1938

This sideboard was manufactured by the Herman Miller Company, which was an important Modern pioneer.

$3,000–$4,000

Machine Age 1925–1940

Largely an American phenomenon, the machine aesthetic was a defining force in design in the years between the two World Wars. Industrial designers applied the principles of aerodynamics to the design of common household objects, providing them with a sense of speed and motion. Machine-Age aerodynamic streamlining was evident in a vast array of products, such as trains, cars, toasters, vacuum cleaners, and salt and pepper shakers.

Many collectors of American Machine Age focus on smaller objects such as cocktail shakers, clocks, and other utilitarian pieces rather than furniture. There are, however, many excellent examples of Machine Age furniture by such designers as Ken Weber, Gilbert Rohde, Norman Bel Geddes, and Frank Lloyd Wright.

SKYSCRAPER CABINET, c. 1935

A powerful example of the influence of skyscrapers on American design, this cabinet by an unknown designer fetched $24,000 at auction.

$20,000–$25,000

SOFA SET, c. 1940

Not always expensive, Machine-Age Modern, like this sofa set by the St. Louis Display Company, was accessible to a large segment of the American public.

$2,000-$4,000 the set

THEATER DOORS, c. 1940

Like many Modernists, Warren McArthur often designed entire installations, including furniture, lighting, and architectural elements such as this door. Many of these unique and expressive pieces are highly sought after by today's collectors.

$3,000–$5,000

AIRLINE CHAIR, c. 1935

This chair is a good example of the uniquely American aesthetic of streamline Modern. The confluence of aerodynamic principles with common household objects gave such items as chairs, toasters and radios a sense of energetic forward motion.

$8,000–$12,000

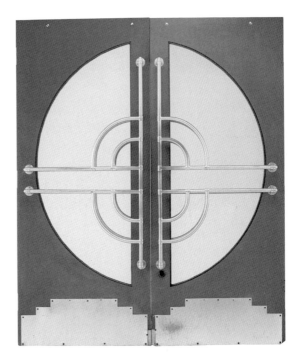

Studio Furniture 1945–1975

In contrast to the enthusiastic partnership that developed between many Modern designers and postwar American technology, there were those who, in the manner of Morris and Ruskin, shunned the machine and returned to a more organic model. Heavily influenced by the life and work of Wharton Esherick, the creators of studio furniture blurred the boundaries between art and furniture. Unhindered by corporate sponsorship, these artists challenged the very definition of furniture with their sculptural masterpieces and their superb craftsmanship.

Studio furniture is one of the fastest growing areas of Modern collecting. Prices for great examples have risen dramatically in recent years. Important Wharton Esherick pieces regularly soar into the high five-figure range, while even average examples of Paul Evans and George Nakashima can bring significant prices at auction.

PAUL EVANS WALL COLLAGE, c. 1965
This signature Evans piece exemplifies the designer's powerful use of sculptural elements to create a dramatic impact.
$4,000–$6,000

WENDELL CASTLE LECTERN, c. 1965
Biomorphic forms are a common feature of studio furniture. This sinuous Castle lectern brought $6,000 at auction.
$4,000–$8,000

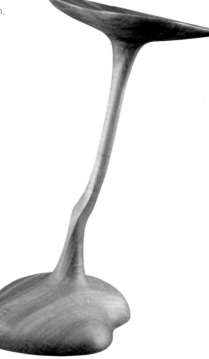

GEORGE NAKASHIMA CONOID TABLES,
(right & below), c. 1966

The use of wildly expressive woods and butterfly joints greatly increases the value of George Nakashima tables and other furniture pieces.
$20,000–$30,000

Butterfly joint

PHILLIP LLOYD POWELL NEW HOPE CHAIR, c. 1958

The New Hope chair demonstrates Powell's ability to combine great Modern design with the beauty of natural materials to produce chairs in the very best handcrafted tradition of studio furniture.
$2,000–$4,000

Postwar 1945–1960

The style most readily associated with postwar Modernism is found in the designs manufactured by the Knoll and Herman Miller companies. These design giants harnessed the creative genius of such people as Charles and Ray Eames, Florence Knoll, Eero Saarinen, George Nelson, Harry Bertoia and Isamu Noguchi to produce Modern furniture for a modern world. These designers and manufacturers developed innovative technologies and radical new materials to meet the challenges of a changing interior environment. Eames pioneered the use of molded plywood, Harry Bertoia designed chairs made of wire mesh, and Eero Saarinen explored the use of plastic in furniture design, all with great success.

Like many of their predecessors, these new Modernists wanted to provide the masses with good design, and like the industrial designers of the 1930s, they hoped to harness the productive power of the machine to meet their goal.

Postwar Modern exemplifies the best of what Modern is. Extremely popular with designers and collectors, postwar Modern can be integrated into almost any interior.

EAMES STORAGE UNIT 400, c. 1954
For many serious collectors, the ESU 400 is the very definition of postwar Modern. Rare and valuable, ESU 400s have sold for as much as $70,000 at auction, though $10,000–$20,000 is the usual auction estimate.
$10,000–$20,000

GEORGE NELSON THIN EDGE SIDEBOARD, c. 1957
The thin-edge series is very popular with today's collectors. Prized for their sophisticated design and use of beautiful woods, these pieces can still be purchased for modest prices at auction.
$2,500–$4,500

HANS WEGNER DINING ROOM SET,
c. 1961

Danish design became very popular during the 1950s and retains its appeal today. Pieces such as this dining-room set by Hans Wegner command high prices in today's market.
$20,000–$30,000 the set

GEORGE NELSON SWAG-LEG DESK,
c. 1960

Swag-leg desks like this one were primarily used in residential settings.
$3,500–$4,000

Pop 1960–1970

Like so many other aspects of society, furniture design in the 1960s experienced a period of profound exploration and self-examination. Furniture designers developed a sense of liberation, a newfound freedom. They challenged conventional notions of design and turned artistic vision into a platform in which to reflect, observe and influence ongoing popular culture. Furniture became a showcase for political and social commentary, and like the art and music of the time, much of the design vocabulary was aimed at engaging the public in a larger dialogue.

Designers such as Olivier Morgue, Gaetano Pesce and Pierre Paulin teamed up with business innovators like Charles Stendig to bring to the public a wide range of challenging Modern furniture.

Despite (or perhaps because of) its excesses, Pop furniture is much sought after by today's collectors. Many people are captivated by the youthful exuberance and raw energy of Pop furniture, which remains relatively inexpensive.

CACTUS COATRACK, c. 1970

Imported into the United States by Charles Stendig, this Gufram Cactus Coatrack never really caught on with the American public.
$3,000–$5,000

EERO AARNIO BALL CHAIR, c. 1965

The ball chair is extremely popular with today's collectors, often finding its way into children's rooms.
$2,000–$4,000

WENDELL CASTLE MOLAR CHAIRS, c. 1969

Castle's witty Molar chairs embody the spirit of Pop furniture—irreverent, humorous, culturally aware and certainly never dull. $3,000–$4,000

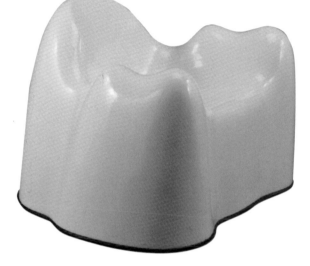

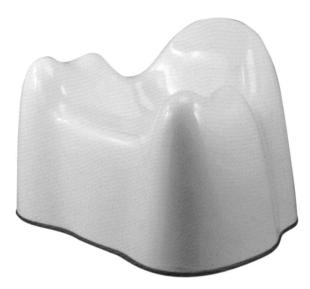

GAVINA "MAGRITTE" CHAIR, c. 1970

As this "Magritte" chair by Gavina makes clear, nothing was too far out during the 1960s. This held true for furniture design as well as the larger worlds of art and architecture. $3,000–$4,000

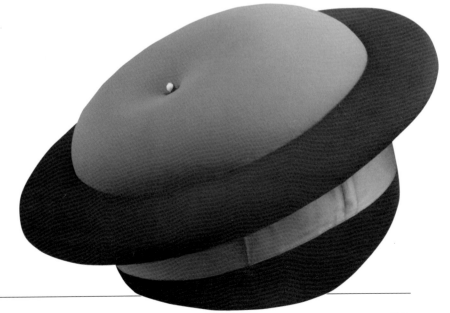

Postmodern 1980–Present

The design style of the Postmodern movement is free-spirited, frivolous, and consciously eclectic, a purposeful and carefully planned burst of artistic spontaneity. In a fast-paced world that reveres technology, and possesses a very limited attention span, Postmodern design was the perfect vehicle to muscle attention from a public suffering from severe sensory overload.

Designers like Gaetano Pesce, Martio Botta, Michael Graves and Ettore Sottsass employed bright colors and contrived forms to shock the public into noticing their furniture. Craftsmen such as Wendell Castle, Albert Palley and Ron Arad used their work to reexamine the look of studio furniture, successfully integrating a strong studio component into Postmodern Design.

Giving their imagination and creativity free reign, Postmodern designers continue to push the envelope of furniture design. Collectors of contemporary art seem to be especially drawn to Postmodern furniture.

WENDELL CASTLE BRIDGE BUFFET, c. 1990
One of America's most important and notable Modern and Postmodern designers, Wendell Castle has been instrumental in the resurgence of an American studio movement.
$12,000–$15,000

ALFONSE MATTIA RACOON BENCH, c. 1990
Unfettered by any design vocabulary, Postmodernists are free to explore the limits of their creative imagination.
$2,000–$4,000

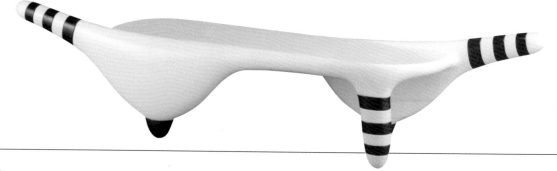

THE FACT FILES

The Fact Files are the heart of this book. These sections are intended to provide the collector with a brief biographical sketch of each highlighted designer, a photo display featuring examples of each designer's most prominent work and helpful collector hints located in "What to Look For" boxes.

One of the challenges facing Modern enthusiasts is the overwhelming amount of material that is classified and collected as "Modern." Unlike many areas of collecting that tend to focus on tight, well-defined time periods, Modernism encompasses the entire 20th century. The Modern collector is unfettered by the constraints of geography. Collecting Modern is a truly international passion. Americans collect French Art Deco. The English collect Bauhaus. The Japanese have a deep appreciation for the work of Charles and Ray Eames.

This worldwide pursuit requires the collector or dealer to have a competent working knowledge of material ranging from the workshops of Vienna, the Deco cabinetmakers of Paris, the icons of American Postwar design, Scandinavian furniture production and the avant-garde masterpieces of the Postmodern movement. Modernism covers 100 years, dozens of countries, several major and often conflicting movements, and a host of various and unlikely materials—a lot to take in and digest. The Fact Files attempt to shed a little bit of light on a very large and wide-ranging subject.

Although the theories and beliefs represented by the Modern movement manifest themselves in many forms, for reasons of practical necessity, this book concentrates on furniture. The furniture covered in these Fact Files must be viewed in the greater context of the artistic expression of this

The Fact Files in this Insider's Guide *survey Modernism's impact on basic furniture types—seating, tables, and storage pieces—as well as on lamps and clocks.*

century. Textiles, ceramics, glassware, fine art and sculpture are all important in the overall fabric of Modern design. The compilation of these diverse forms produces a Modern tapestry that helps to define and recall the imagination, drama and excitement of the 20th century.

With the tremendous diversity that is Modernism, choosing individual designers for inclusion in these Fact Files was a daunting task. Many well-known designers have been omitted purposely, with attention given to more obscure, yet historically significant, figures. Special attention has also been given to those people who are up-and-coming in the Modern arena. The sensuously crafted work of Phil Powell is a perfect example. Although not well-known outside East Coast collecting circles, his work demonstrates the contribution of the studio furniture movement to the 20th century mix. Particular emphasis was placed on the Postmodernists as their work is still young in the marketplace. Great designs by Ron Arad, Gaetano Pesce and Wendell Castle are often available on the secondary market for a fraction

of their original cost decades ago, offering the collector good investment opportunities.

One of the most difficult aspects of producing these Fact Files was determining values for various pieces. The Modern market can be fickle and prices can vary by region. Eames may bring more in Los Angeles, Parzinger may be in greater demand in Chicago and Nakashima may bring more in New York. At best, this makes pricing an imprecise affair. Interest waxes and wanes with the latest trends. If you paid more than an item is listed for here, don't feel that you've been taken advantage of. These values are meant to serve as a general guide—they are not written in stone because the market is still young. Since its inception, Modernism's primary call has been to imagination and risk. Learn and enjoy!

Phil Powell's woodwork, such as this cabinet and lamp, c. 1956, exemplifies excellence in modern form and craft.

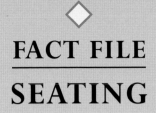

The history of Modern design can be chronicled by the evolution of the chair. Modern designers have long relied on chairs to communicate their most radical design notions and to define the fundamental beliefs, concepts and possibilities of the Modern movement. By observing the developments and changes in chair design throughout the 20th century, the student of Modernism can develop a clear appreciation for the nuances of design history.

In this century, chairs have been used to challenge the architectural and aesthetic status quo. Chairs have employed unconventional engineering techniques, utilized non traditional materials and had their basic forms altered in ordered to influence static design concepts or as a vehicle for larger social commentary. The chair has become the most interpreted of any furniture form, acting as intermediary between the creative intent of the designer and the reality of consumer and marketplace.

The designers highlighted in this section are some of the most historically significant of the Modern movement. Their contributions form the foundations on which Modernism is built. Many similarities as well as profound differences are evident in the work of these designers. People like Harry Bertoia and Edward Wormley worked for large corporate interests for pay and promise. Studio artists like George Nakashima and Phil Powell were never sure what was around the next economic corner. Florence Knoll designed innovative furniture and was instrumental in the development of one of America's most influential furniture manufacturer and distributors —the Knoll Company.

These designers' approaches to the stylistic and aesthetic challenges of chair design could not have been more diverse. Phil Powell harnessed the beauty of American black walnut to capture the imagination, while Gaetano Pesce and the Postmodernists used plastics, resins and steel to the same end. Frank Lloyd Wright relied on geometry with its crisp angles and clean lines to communicate his vision of design harmony. Edward Wormley mixed modernized forms with neoclassical influences to produce furniture that inspired the marketplace for decades.

Understanding the development of the chair is critical to understanding the larger issues of Modernism and its history.

Florence Knoll

Fine design and attention to detail are never absent from anything created by Florence Knoll. In 1943, Florence Schust was hired by Hans Knoll to oversee the development of textile designs for Knoll Associates, the furniture company he had founded in 1938. Their design collaboration became personal as well when they married in 1946.

Florence Knoll's talent had been recognized and encouraged early on by Eliel Saarinen at the Cranbrook Academy of Art in Michigan. Knoll's keen sense of the Modern aesthetic was honed through her architecture studies with notable teachers like Mies van der Rohe, Walter Gropius and Marcel Breuer. All of these experiences gave her understanding of Modernism a remarkable depth and scope.

The Knolls were especially adept at creating an environment in which creativity could flourish. Florence Knoll surrounded herself with the best and brightest of the time, attracting such designers as Harry Bertoia, Isamu Noguchi and Eero Saarinen to invest their time and talent with the young company.

Florence Knoll's vision extended from the corporate boardroom to the living room at home. She created a new way of using office space—the open modular plan—and designed the furniture to fill it. Walk into any major corporate office today and her influence is still visible.

Every detail of a Knoll piece was meticulously considered. Handles, wood grain, textiles, finishes and colors came under Knoll's scrutiny. Knoll designed for interiors and created interiors to go with designs. Her versatility and creativity served the company well, and it rapidly grew into an international success. Florence Knoll's design clients read like a Who's Who of 1950s corporate America. She did interiors for the Rockefeller family offices in Rockefeller Plaza, Connecticut General Life Insurance Company (her first large-scale effort),

LEATHER SOFA,
c. 1960
Knoll furniture can often be identified by its spare lines and boxy design.
$3,000–$4,000

H.J. Heinz offices, the CBS building and Knoll showrooms in the United States and abroad.

Knoll furniture is accessible and collectible. The large quantities produced make the prices attractive to entry-level collectors. Signature pieces like Knoll's conference table bring between $2,000 and $3,000 depending on the veneers used. Knoll catalogs are available to document pieces and attribute them to various designers for Knoll Associates.

WHAT TO LOOK FOR:

◆ chrome legs
◆ exterior chrome frames
◆ boxy design
◆ excellent construction
◆ often found in used office furniture stores

ARMCHAIR,
c. 1960
Original fabric enhances the value of this Knoll chair.
$3,000–$4,000

Button tufting is common on many Knoll designs.

PAIR OF EASY CHAIRS, c. 1954
Knoll furniture was very popular with contract designers and is often found in commercial settings.
$650–$950 each

Harry Bertoia

The principles of Modernism and motion were combined by Harry Bertoia to produce some of the 20th century's most distinctive industrial and artistic forms. Jewelry, sculptures and furniture designed by Bertoia all evidence a grace and fluidity as well as the clean edges characteristic of the Modern movement. Italian by birth, Bertoia came to the United States. He studied at the Cranbrook Academy of Art from 1937 to 1939 and taught jewelry making and metalworking there between 1939 and 1943. His jewelry and monoprints were met with great enthusiasm by the public and are found in many prestigious collections around the world. Between the years 1943 and 1947, he worked with Charles and Ray Eames, designing furniture at Evans Products and Plyform Products. In 1950, he became a designer for Knoll, where he created his iconic wire-mesh Diamond chair. Fifty years later, no textbook on Modernism fails to include this most important contribution to the movement, and yet Bertoia's great passion was sculpture.

His sculptures (*see page 48*) invite all of the senses to participate in their appreciation. Most of them move when touched by wind or human hands, and make percussive sounds or musical tones. Sculpture commissions dominated Bertoia's work during the

DIAMOND CHAIRS,
c. 1950
These come in two sizes—shown here are the larger lounge chairs.
$600–$900 each

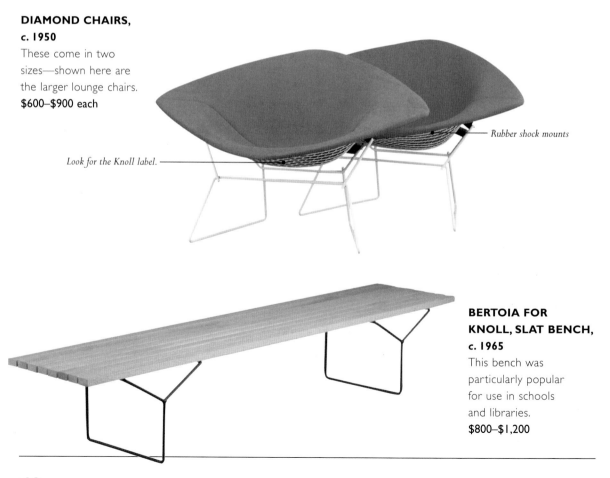

Look for the Knoll label.

Rubber shock mounts

BERTOIA FOR KNOLL, SLAT BENCH,
c. 1965
This bench was particularly popular for use in schools and libraries.
$800–$1,200

1960s. These ranged from very small, whimsical forms to large pieces designed for public spaces. During the late 1960s and 1970s he continued to produce sculpture, a small number of monoprints and even reprised his role as a jewelry maker on a very limited basis.

Bertoia's work is highly sought after because of his unique contributions to modern design. His work is accessible to every level of the marketplace. Diamond chairs are readily available and reasonable in price. Sculptures range from $5,000 to the low six figures. Monoprints have recently drawn the interest of collectors and range in price from $1,000 to $15,000. Jewelry is scarce and brings premium prices.

It is important for collectors to note that Bertoia signed neither his sculptures nor his monoprints. Therefore provenance or documentation through catalogs or books is of critical importance.

WHAT TO LOOK FOR:

- white, black or chrome bases—chrome is usually the most desirable
- broken wires or loose wires—these cut values by as much as half
- cover in good shape and bright colors adds to the value
- shock mounts intact and in good shape
- Knoll stickers on the bottom of seat covers

BIRD CHAIR & OTTOMAN, c. 1947
A favorite among collectors, and much more comfortable than it looks. Manufactured by Knoll.
$1,000–$1,500

Check shock mounts for damage.

BERTOIA SCULPTURES

Harry Bertoia's furniture may be well known to the Modern collector because of the popularity of his wire-mesh Diamond chairs, but furniture design really played a secondary role to his sculpture. Bertoia's pieces are highly diverse in size and style. Some seem organic, others suggest the industrial. In fact, he straddled the worlds of handicraft and industry and was equally at ease in functional and non-functional design, working on a small scale or filling commissions for monumental sculpture. Some of his sculptures are site specific, made for residential or commercial interiors or public spaces. Some produced sounds when moved and invited the viewer to touch them, others were more angular and static.

Bertoia's sculptures have recently come to the fore of Modern art. They are appreciated not only by collectors of Modern furniture, but also by art lovers. Smaller tabletop works can bring as little as $1,000, while larger freestanding sculptures have sold in the high five-figure range. Some Bertoia sculptures were produced in fairly large editions and bring far less than one-of-a-kind pieces.

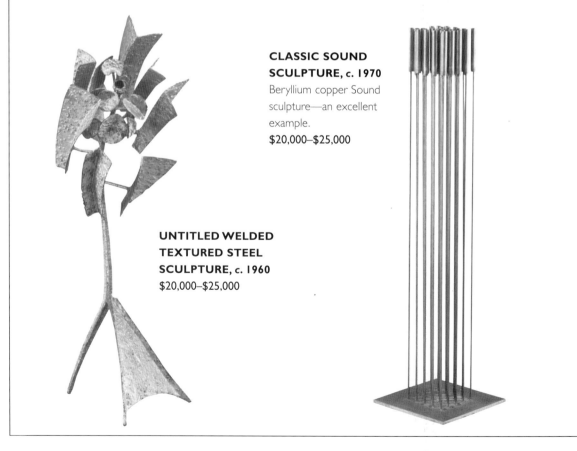

CLASSIC SOUND SCULPTURE, *c.* 1970
Beryllium copper Sound sculpture—an excellent example.
$20,000–$25,000

UNTITLED WELDED TEXTURED STEEL SCULPTURE, *c.* 1960
$20,000–$25,000

EUROPEAN ROOTS

The Modern movement began as a struggle against the oppressive and dehumanizing effects of industrialization on art and design. As the 19th century drew to a close, furniture design in particular had become an unimaginative and formulaic affair. Commercial furniture manufacturers turned out ever greater quantities of cheap, machine-made copies of earlier styles for a clientele with a taste for richness and ornament.

Encouraged by the writings of John Ruskin and William Morris, who looked to the Middle Ages for inspiration for their designs and production methods, communities of craftspeople sprang up in the United Kingdom and across Europe, championing handcraftsmanship and the unity of architecture and the decorative arts. Their guilds and publications gave rise to the Arts and Crafts movement.

As the Arts and Crafts movement gained momentum, another group of reformers, organized in Vienna by Josef Hoffmann and Koloman Moser, publicly seceded from the conservative *Kunstgewerbeschule* in 1897 and became known as the Secessionists. Like John Ruskin and William Morris, the Secessionists reacted against the dehumanizing effects of industrialization. In contrast to Morris, however, who turned nostalgically to an imagined vision of a Medieval past, the Secessionists did an amazing thing. They looked forward. Led by Hoffmann and Moser, and inspired by the influential Scottish architect and designer Charles Rennie Mackintosh, the Secessionists replaced excessive decoration with simple geometric shapes and restrained ornament. They also advocated a total environment in which architecture, interior design and furniture constituted a unified aesthetic whole.

At the end of World War I, two design movements took root in Europe and spread rapidly as international styles. In Paris, the opulent Art Deco style continued the traditions of 18th-century French cabinetmakers. Its hallmarks were the use of rich materials, bold color schemes and such decorative patterns as zig-zags, circles, lightening bolts and pyramids. At the same time, the theory of Functionalism was being tested at the Bauhaus in Weimar, Germany. Although complete aesthetic opposites, these two styles—Bauhaus and Art Deco—would influence furniture design for the rest of the century and beyond.

Charles Rennie Mackintosh

ARGYLE STREET HIGH-BACK CHAIR, c. 1896

One of the best known of all Mackintosh designs, this rare high-back, dark-stained oak chair was made for Mrs. Cranston's Argyle Street tea rooms in Glasgow. The first of Mackintosh's high-back chairs, this design features an oval on the back rail with a stylized flying bird design cut through it. The seats were either rush or upholstered with horsehair. Mackintosh used this chair in his own flat and exhibited several of them in Vienna in 1900.
$200,000–$300,000

CHARLES RENNIE MACKINTOSH

CHEST, c. 1903

This ebonized-pine toy chest with recessed aluminum plaques was one of a pair Mackintosh gave his godson. $3,000–$4,000

DESK, c. 1918

Mackintosh designed this fall-front desk, shown open (below right) and closed (below), for the Blue Bedroom of William Blackie's palatial Hill House. If it came on the auction market today, the Hill House desk could bring well over $500,000.

Gerrit Rietveld

INSIDER'S INFORMATION

The Dutch furniture designer and architect Gerrit Rietveld sought to reduce furniture pieces to their most elemental planes and angles so they would stand out freely and clearly in space. Rietveld drew inspiration from the work of Charles Rennie Mackintosh and Frank Lloyd Wright, and his association with Piet Mondrian and the De Stijl group of artists is evident in some of his startlingly original furniture designs. In turn, Rietveld's influence would reverberate throughout the 20th century.

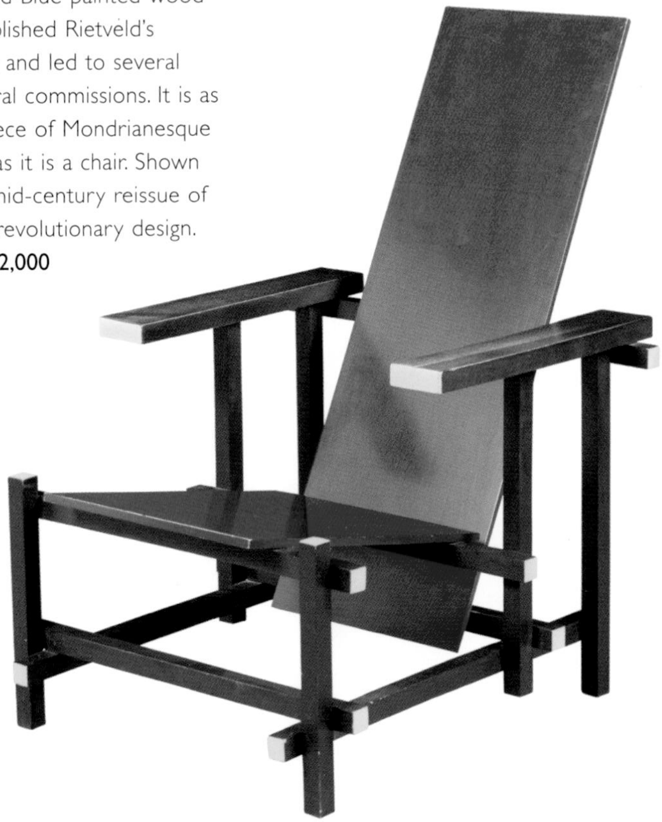

RED-BLUE CHAIR, 1955

Originally designed in 1918, the famous Red-Blue painted wood chair established Rietveld's reputation and led to several architectural commissions. It is as much a piece of Mondrianesque sculpture as it is a chair. Shown here is a mid-century reissue of Rietveld's revolutionary design.

$8,000–$12,000

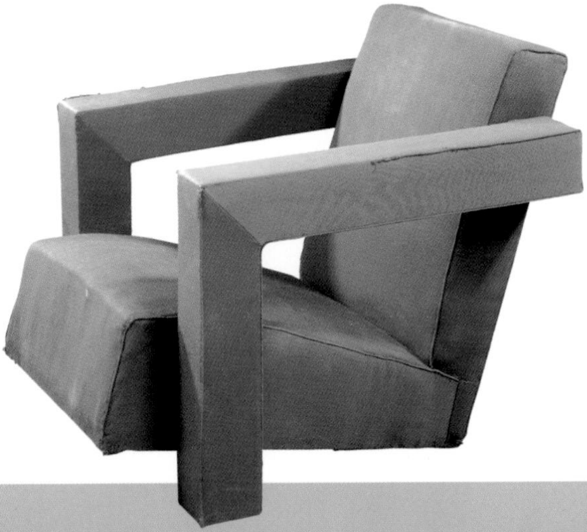

UTRECHT CHAIR, 1935

This upholstered lounge chair is a good example of the low-cost, avant garde furniture Rietveld designed for the Amsterdam department store Metz & Company. The Utrecht chair is still in production today.

ZIG-ZAG CHAIR WITH ARMS, 1934

Improbable as it seems, the Zig-Zag chair's wedged dovetail joints make it quite strong. It was produced in several variations and in fairly large numbers through the 1950s. Zig-Zag chairs with arms are worth considerably more than those without.

$20,000–$40,000 with arms

PROTOTYPE BEUGEL STOEL, 1927

Rietveld's famous molded-plywood Beugel Stoel, a very early example of the use of plywood in furniture-making, is shown here in a rare prototype. Such prototypes bring a premium in the marketplace.

$20,000–$30,000

Josef Hoffmann

ROUND TABLE, *c.* 1908

The clean lines and ball decorations of this beechwood-and-brass table, manufactured by the Vienna firm of Jacob & Joseph Kohn, are hallmarks of Hoffmann's designs.

$2,000–$4,000

TABLE LAMP, *c.* 1905

A classic Wiener Werkstätte object, this Hoffmann lamp consists of a simple silvered-metal base and glass-bead shade.

$50,000–$70,000

SITZMASCHINE CHAIR, MODEL 670, *c.* 1905

Hoffmann designed one of his most famous pieces, the "sitting machine" reclining chair, for a nursing home near Vienna, the Purckersdorf Sanatorium, which he also designed. Manufactured by Jacob & Joseph Kohn, the chair is made of stained, steam-bent beechwood, with a plywood seat, a geometric pierced adjustable back and bentwood arms. Some models, like this one, included a footrest.

$25,000–$30,000

INSIDER'S INFORMATION

Josef Hoffmann was a founding member of the Vienna Secession movement (1897) and of the Wiener Werkstätte (Vienna Workshop), which lasted from 1903 through 1932. This community of artists, designers, and craftspeople had as its goal the fusion of architecture and the decorative arts into an aesthetic whole and the promotion of craftsmanship at its highest levels. Influenced by the work of Charles Rennie Mackintosh, Hoffmann's austere, rectilinear furniture pieces are enriched with cutouts and decorative balls. Although Hoffmann's roots were in Art Nouveau, the purity and clarity of his later designs make him an important figure in the evolution of 20th-century Modernism.

BOOKCASE, c. 1912
Hoffmann's monumental bookcase is made of oak and ebonized wood with glass doors. Its classic proportions and restrained decorative details were designed to complement the architecture of the room for which it was intended.
$30,000–$40,000

BENTWOOD CHAIRS, c. 1904
These elegant bentwood chairs were designed by Hoffmann for the Purckersdorf Sanatorium and executed by Jacob & Joseph Kohn.
$50,000–$90,000 the pair

Marcel Breuer

bt24 ARMCHAIR, c. 1930
Even with its upholstery in poor
condition, this rare Breuer design has
great appeal for today's collectors.
$5,000–$7,000

**BRYN MAWR DESK AND
CHAIRS, c. 1937**
Breuer designed this desk and pair
of chairs for Bryn Mawr College,
in Pennsylvania. Their sleek lines and
hard edges brought a taste of
Bauhaus style to America.
Desk **$2,000–$4,000**
Chairs **$3,000–$4,000** each

CHAISE LONGUE, c. 1935

Originally designed for the Isokon
company, this Breuer chaise longue
was later manufactured by Knoll.
The Knoll examples bring
considerably less at auction.
$6,000–$9,000

BRYN MAWR CHEST OF DRAWERS, c. 1937

Breuer's first major American
commission, the Bryn Mawr suite
also included this large chest of
drawers as well as a shelving unit
and a long rectangular mirror.
$3,000–$4,000

Ludwig Mies van der Rohe

MR10 CHAIR, 1927
This classic Mies van der Rohe design exemplifies Modernism's "form follows function" ideal.
$3,000–$4,000

MR90 CHAIRS, 1929
The iconic Barcelona chair is considered this Modern master's signature design.
$1,500–$2,000 each

DAYBED, 1930

Originally designed for the Tugendhat House in Brünn (Czech Republic), this elegant daybed is still much in demand both in its vintage version and in the Knoll reissue.

$4,000–$6,000 Knoll reissue

MR20 ARMCHAIR, 1927

Mies van der Rohe, along with Mart Stam and Marcel Breuer, pioneered the use of tubular metal in Modern furniture.

$5,000–$7,000

French Art Deco

EMILE DUGAY FURNITURE SUITE, c. 1925

Dugay designed this magnificent ensemble for the Château de Grenay. The mahogany-and-leather chairs, mahogany-and-marble table, and mahogany pedestal and sconces are typical of high-style French Art Deco of the mid-1920s.

Chairs $15,000–$20,000 the pair
Table $8,000–$12,000
Pedestal $8,000–$12,000
Chrome and peach-glass lamp $600–$900
Bronzed-terra-cotta sculpture $800–$1,200

Sconces $3,000–$4,000

ALBERT CHEURET TABLE LAMP, c. 1925

This bronze and alabaster lamp is a superb example of the geometric rendering of natural forms typical of French Art Deco in general and of Cheuret's design in particular.
$15,000–$20,000

EDGAR BRANDT TIERED CEILING LIGHT, c. 1925

Edgar Brandt was the master of Art Deco ironwork. This wrought-iron ceiling light features a Daum acid-etched glass shade.
$15,000–$20,000

EDGAR BRANDT SCONCE, c. 1925

Usually sold in pairs, this elaborate sconce was made of wrought iron and either alabaster or Daum glass.
$8,000–$12,000 each
$25,000–$30,000 for a pair

Le Corbusier

INSIDER'S INFORMATION

Born Charles Edouard Jeanneret in Switzerland in 1887, the man who would become one of the 20th century's greatest design visionaries changed his name to Le Corbusier in Paris in 1920, when he co-founded the magazine *L'Esprit Nouveau* to publicize his theories. A key figure in the development of the International style of the 1920s, Le Corbusier championed the use of modern industrial materials and standardized, mass-produced functional furniture for industrial-age houses he dubbed "machines for living." Le Corbusier's influence on 20th-century architecture, urban-planning and furniture design cannot be overestimated.

BASCULANT ARMCHAIR, c. 1928

An International Style icon, the chrome-plated tubular-steel Basculant chair was designed by Le Corbusier in association with his cousin Pierre Jeanneret and Charlotte Perriand. Originally manufactured by Thonet, the influential B301 has been reissued by Cassina as part of its 20th-century Classics line.
$15,000–$25,000

DINING TABLE, 1929

Le Corbusier's designs for his Cité de Refuge de L'Armée du Salut—the Salvation Army center—in Paris included this table made of light blue painted steel, wood and linoleum.
$10,000–$20,000

TUBULAR STEEL ARMCHAIR, 1932

A rare, hand-built tubular steel armchair, codesigned by Le Corbusier and Charlotte Perriand. Many of Le Corbusier's furniture designs, such as this chair and the kitchen unit below, were collaborative efforts with Perriand and Pierre Jeanneret. Attributing and valuing such pieces is difficult.

TYPE I KITCHEN UNIT, 1952

A Painted wood-and-aluminum Type I kitchen unit executed by Atelier Le Corbusier specifically for the *Unité d' Habitation*, Le Corbusier's highly influential public-housing apartment block in Marseilles, France.

Alvar Aalto

DINING-ROOM SET, c.1940
The simplicity and functionality of Aalto designs are evident in this straightforward birchwood dining-room set.
$4,000–$6,000

DORMITORY STUDY/STORAGE UNIT, c. 1951
Aalto designed this innovative spiraling desk and shelving unit for the Massachusetts Institute of Technology.
$3,000–$4,000

MODEL NO. 69 DINETTE SUITE, c. 1960
Although originally designed in 1933, the Model No. 69 dinette table and chairs looked far from dated when this set was produced in 1960.
$1,500–$2,500

Edward Wormley

Edward Wormley was a prodigious designer whose collaboration with the Dunbar Furniture Company produced elegant, sophisticated modern furniture for almost four decades.

As a young man, Wormley worked as an interior designer for the upscale department store Marshall Fields. In 1931, he met Homer Niederhauser, the president of the Dunbar Furniture Company of Berne, Indiana. Dunbar was producing mostly upholstered furniture that drew its inspiration from colonial designs. Niederhauser wanted to upgrade and modernize the company's product line and hired the young Wormley to direct the effort.

Wormley quickly added a line of Modern furniture to Dunbar's traditional interiors. In 1944, as a result of the tremendous success of the Modern line, Dunbar eliminated all traditional furniture from its catalogs.

In 1944 Wormley moved to New York and opened his own design office, but continued to design for Dunbar as an independent consultant instead of as an employee. He also designed furniture for the Drexel Company, globe stands for Rand McNally and textiles for Schiffer Prints.

The magnitude of Wormley's design output was staggering. He often would produce two or more collections each year for Dunbar. His success was the result of his ability to translate the hard-edged vocabulary of Modern into livable, inviting residential furniture that appealed to a more conservative but still sophisticated clientele.

In 1957 Wormley designed what would become one of his most successful lines and the one most sought after by today's collectors—the Janus line. Inspired by the work of California Arts and Crafts designers Greene and Greene, the line featured

Mix of fabric and exposed wood

Looped legs

PAIR OF JANUS CHAIRS AND A LONG BENCH, c. 1958
The Janus series is among the most sought after by collectors.
Chair $1,500–$2,000 each
Table $1,500–$2,000

pieces studded with Tiffany and Natzler tiles.

Today, Wormley's Dunbar furniture is highly desired by both collectors and designers who appreciate its timeless sophistication, its urban aesthetic and its superior craftsmanship. Pieces that have Natzler or Tiffany tiles are of extreme interest and bring significant prices. Other pieces that collectors are on the lookout for include Wormley's Listen-to-Me chaise and La Gondola sofas. Dunbar also produced a small number of custom pieces for Wormley's clients. These are rare and valuable.

WHAT TO LOOK FOR:

◆ excellent construction techniques
◆ Dunbar labeling integrated into the decking of upholstered furniture
◆ brass caps on furniture feet
◆ fine detailing

WING CHAIR AND OTTOMAN, c. 1960
These sophisticated pieces illustrate

Wormley's ability to modernize traditional styles.
$1,700–$2,000

Look for Dunbar label on decking beneath cushion.

Original fabric

TETE-A-TETE FOR DUNBAR, c.1965
This is an extremely rare Wormley form. The

original fabric on this example makes it even more valuable.
$6,000–$8,000

DINING CHAIRS,
c. 1955
The fine craftsmanship of Dunbar furniture is rare in production pieces.
$2,000–$3,000

GONDOLA SOFA,
c. 1959
$3,500–$4,500

Original silk fabric

Look for Dunbar label on decking beneath cushion.

UPHOLSTERED ARMCHAIRS ON ROSEWOOD BASE, LATE 1950s
Dunbar furniture was expensive when originally sold and today is often found in some of America's most exclusive homes.
$1,200–$1,500 each

An
regula
bench
inclu
and b

B
custc
vers
his c
seer
back
tap
con

1,0
car
qu
$1
in

N
I
T
c
s
t
a
l

George Nakashima

George Nakashima's wide-ranging experience brought a sense of life and adventure into his work. His inspiration came from a search for truth that sent him all over the world in pursuit of answers.

In 1931, after earning a Master's degree in architecture from M.I.T., Nakashima sold his car and purchased a round-the-world tramp steamship ticket. He spent a year in France living the life of a bohemian, then went on to North Africa and eventually to Japan. While in Japan, Nakashima went to work for Antonin Raymond, an American architect who had collaborated with Frank Lloyd Wright on the Imperial Hotel. While working for Raymond, Nakashima toured Japan extensively, studying the subtleties of Japanese architecture and design.

In 1937 Raymond's company was commissioned to build a dormitory at an ashram in Pondicherry, India, for which Nakashima was the primary construction consultant. It was here that Nakashima made his first furniture.

In 1940 Nakashima returned to America and began to teach woodworking and to make furniture in Seattle. Like others of Japanese ancestry, he was interned at Camp Minidoka, in Hunt, Idaho, in March 1942. At the camp, he met a man trained in traditional Japanese carpentry, and learned to approach woodworking with discipline and patience, striving for perfection in every stage of construction.

In 1943 Antonin Raymond successfully sponsored Nakashima's release from the camp and invited him to his farm in New Hope, Pennsylvania. In his studio and workshop at New Hope, Nakashima explored the organic expressiveness of wood, choosing boards with knots and burls and figured grain. Drawing on Japanese designs and shop practices, as well as on American and International Modern styles, Nakashima created a body of work that would make his name synonymous with the best of mid-century studio furniture.

THE LONG CHAIR, 1958

Early examples of Nakashima's work do not necessarily command higher prices than more recent ones. His genius flourished with age.

$6,000–$7,000

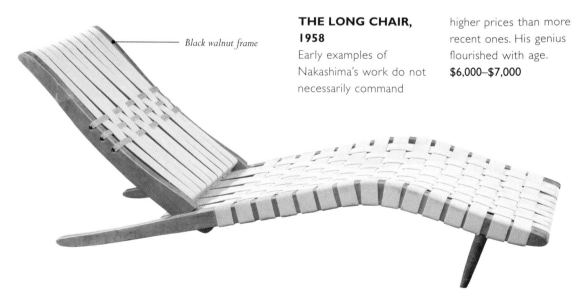

Black walnut frame

WHAT TO LOOK FOR:

- black walnut chairs and benches
- free-form boards
- hand-hewn hickory spindles.
- provenance—Nakashima pieces are seldom signed so provenance is important

GREENROCK STOOLS, c. 1970

A commonly found Nakishima form. These examples were intended for Greenrock, a Rockefeller estate, and their cushions are covered with antique Japanese fabric. These factors plus excellent condition pushed their price at auction to $21,000 (the pair). Greenrock stools generally bring **$2,000–$3,000 each**

Hand-carved spindles

CONOID CUSHION CHAIR, c. 1965

One of George Nakishima's most classic designs. Like all examples of his Conoid group, these pieces have a strong market following. **$5,000–$7,000 each**

CONOID BENCH, c. 1965

A beautiful example of a Nakashima Conoid Bench. **$10,000–$25,000**

Free-form edge

Archizoom Associati

The Italian design group Archizoom was one of a number of collaboratives that surfaced at the end of the 1960s. Like the communes of the same era, these associations were created to explore alternative ideas, usually rejecting the prevailing design philosophy of "form follows function." Young designers were increasingly becoming disillusioned with "good design," and used new materials, such as dense polyurethane foam injection, as well as the more traditional molded plastics to create bold new forms. Archizoom's design team, which included Andrea Branzi and Paolo Deganello, were among the first radical designers to rebel against established Modernist principles by introducing forms infused with irony and a Pop-kitsch sensibility.

The Safari seating unit was designed for an upscale luxury market. An advertising campaign for the product dared the consumer to be selfish and to indulge in the "personal experience of the modular livingscape." The Joe sofa, named for American baseball legend Joe DiMaggio, is a typical design of the 1960s in that it not only refers to a popular culture celebrity, but also pays homage to the work of a leading fine artist—in this case Claes Oldenburg—by making a common object larger-than-life size. Just as the Pop artists were challenging what could be accepted as "fine art," furniture designers such as Mario Cecchi, Jonathon DePas, and d'Urbino & Lomazzi were challenging people's perceptions of interior furnishings.

**ARCHIZOOM
ASSOCIATI SAFARI
MODULAR SEATING
SYSTEM, 1968**
Manufactured by
Poltronova.
$15,000–$16,500

*Molded fiberglass with
upholstered foam-rubber seats*

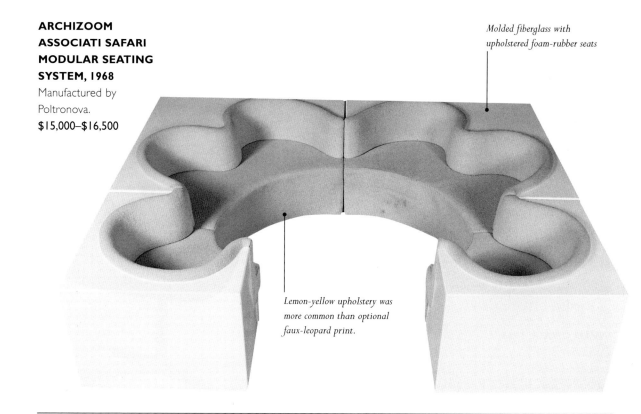

*Lemon-yellow upholstery was
more common than optional
faux-leopard print.*

WHAT TO LOOK FOR:

- ◆ synthetic materials
- ◆ bright primary colors
- ◆ oversize shapes

JOE CHAIR PROTOTYPE, c. 1969

Manufactured by Jonathon DePas, Donato d'Urbino & Paolo Lomazzi.
$8,000–$12,000

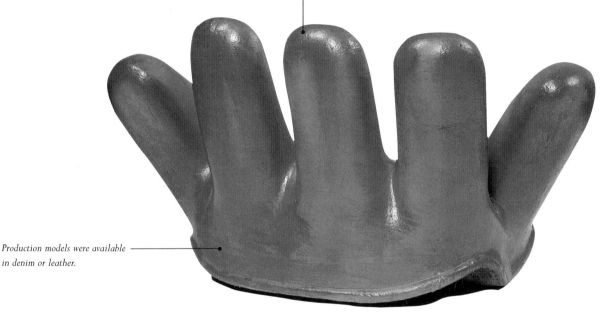

Red self-skinning molded polyurethane foam with internal supports for thumb and fingers.

Production models were available in denim or leather.

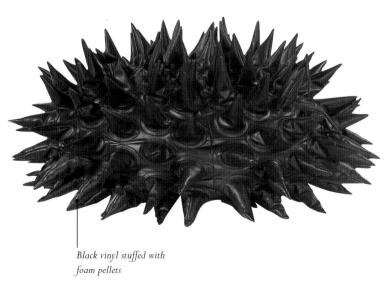

MARIO CECCHI BEAN-BAG CHAIR, 1969

Manufactured by Studio Most. This extremely labor-intensive chair was costly to produce and available for only a short time. It also came in metallic sparkle vinyl.
$5,000–$6,000

Black vinyl stuffed with foam pellets

Frank O. Gehry

One of today's foremost architects, Canadian-born Frank O. Gehry received his training at UCLA and Harvard's Graduate School of Design. He taught architecture at Yale and Harvard for a short period, but he is best known for his landmark architectural commissions, including the Vitra Design Museum and factory in Germany, and the Guggenheim Museum in Bilbao, Spain. In 1989 he was awarded the coveted Pritzker Architecture Prize.

Gehry began designing furniture in 1954. Like his architecture, his furniture designs are eye-opening and innovative. He used inexpensive materials in new ways, rendering them into sculptural forms. Launched in 1972, his Easy Edges line of corrugated cardboard furniture consisted of 17 pieces, including tables, chairs and desks, all made of cardboard. The unexpected combination of high style and lowly material was a surprise hit on the market and brought Gehry into the national limelight. Due to manufacturing and distribution problems, the line was produced for only three months. Gehry revisited cardboard furniture design in the 1980s with a bulkier, shaggier, more expensive line called Rough Edges. In 1987 he introduced the cardboard Bubbles lounge chair. Gehry also designed a series of Fish lamps for Formica, using the company's ColorCore® laminate product, and in 1991, a line of woven bentwood furniture for Knoll, which he used in the dining room of the Guggenheim Museum in Bilbao.

Collectors of Gehry's furniture can expect to pay from $600 to $900 for simpler, smaller forms like an Easy Edges Wiggle sidechair, and up to $6,000 to $8,000 for more complex designs like the Bubbles lounge chair or the Grandpa Beaver chair. Condition is a very important factor in assessing value because of the fragile nature of the material and the fact that once it is damaged it is hard to repair. Look closely for separations, water stains and deterioration of the cardboard—all common condition issues in Gehry furniture. For this reason, Gehry pieces rarely come on the marketplace. Yet, its imaginative, unmistakably American look gives it a special place in collections all over the world.

EASY EDGES ROCKER, c. 1972
A good example of Gehry's innovative use of materials and forms.
$6,000–$7,000

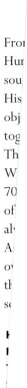

From
Hur
sou
His
obj
tog
Th
W
70
of
al
A
o
th
s

BUBBLES LOUNGE CHAIR, c.1987
This limited-edition corrugated cardboard chair is actually much more comfortable than it looks.
$7,000–$8,000

WHAT TO LOOK FOR:

◆ condition—a critical factor in all of Gehry's cardboard furniture

◆ water stains or other discolorations—these are very difficult to cover or remove

◆ extreme wear around edges or the eroding of backs or sides—such damage considerably lowers value

GRANDPA BEAVER CLUB CHAIR, c. 1987
A prototype child's chair is shown in front of the club chair.
Club chair $4,000–$6,000
Child's chair $1,000–$2,000

homes popular in the 1940s and 50s, even though it had been toned down for more mainstream tastes and is not as angular and exaggerated as some of his earlier work. While Wright's custom furniture was made of solid wood and generally finished by hand, his Heritage-Henredon tables were made of walnut veneer and featured a machine-made Greek key motif around the edges.

Furniture made on commission for Frank Lloyd Wright houses commands high prices. Tables of this sort range from $2,000 to $3,000 and up to the low five figures for unusual pieces. Examples produced by the Heritage-Henredon Company bring considerably less. Occasional and end tables usually range between $1,000 and $2,000; dining tables, between $3,000 and $4,000.

WHAT TO LOOK FOR:

- Frank Lloyd Wright furniture for custom commissions—such pieces are rare and almost never signed
- Wright's furniture signature on his Heritage-Henredon furniture
- walnut veneers and a Greek key motif on Heritage-Henredon pieces

COFFEE TABLE,
c. 1950
Manufactured by
Heritage-Henredon.
$1,400–$1,900

Note the simplicity and clean lines typical of Frank Lloyd Wright design.

EXECUTIVE DESK,
c. 1955
Designed for Wright's
Price Tower Building in
Bartlesville, Oklahoma.
$6,000–$10,000

Edward Wormley

Born in 1907, Edward Wormley left rural Rochelle, Illinois, in 1926 to study briefly at the Art Institute of Chicago. Funds ran out after only a year and a half, and Wormley went to work as an interior designer for Marshall Fields & Company department store. During the Depression, Wormley was introduced to the president of the Dunbar Furniture Company of Berne, Indiana, who hired him to upgrade their product line.

Dunbar made a good choice, as Wormley's work met with immediate success. In 1944 the company decided to focus strictly on Modern lines, and Edward Wormley rose to the task, incorporating European and Scandinavian innovations.

His eye for quality and the exacting craftsmanship at Dunbar made for furniture that was elegant, understated and exceptionally well-made. Wormley was never really at the forefront of Modern design. Instead, he took the best elements from classical, historical design and translated them into the Modern vernacular. The result was furniture that was sophisticated, yet mainstream and very successful.

Wormley's inclusion in the Good Design Exhibitions staged by the Museum of Modern Art and the Merchandise Mart between 1950 and 1955 elevated him to a respected place alongside more cutting-edge designers like Bertoia, Nelson and Eames. Wormley understood the essential elements of Modernism but never limited himself to one ideology. His furniture represented a convergence of historical design and 20th-century innovation that greatly appeals to today's collectors.

Wormley's occasional tables for Dunbar tend to be overshadowed by his wonderful Modern upholstered pieces, but his tile-topped tables created as part of the Janus line in 1957 were a perfect partnership between Modern production design aesthetic and the craft tile tradition of Tiffany and the Natzlers. Dining tables, stacking tables and other occasional tables manufactured by Dunbar have been popular at auction but none have met with the success of these striking examples.

WALNUT COFFEE TABLE WITH NATZLER TILES
c. 1958

Natzler tile inlays in Wormley furniture greatly enhance its value.
$4,000–$6,000

Natzler tile inlay.

THREE-LEGGED TABLES WITH INLAID TIFFANY GLASS MOSAIC, c. 1958

Generally, the most valuable Wormley pieces are those that incorporate Tiffany glass. $10,000–$12,000 each

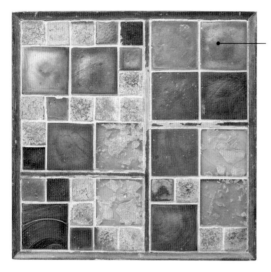

Tiffany glass top

Fine wood construction

WHAT TO LOOK FOR:

◆ complex joinery
◆ brass-capped feet
◆ Dunbar tags and labels
◆ exotic veneers
◆ elliptical and geometric shapes

LIVING ROOM FURNITURE, c. 1955

This grouping is typical of the beauty and sophistication of the designer at his best.

Upholstered side chair $2,000–$3,000
Side table $600–$900
Sideboard $3,000–$4,000

Exotic veneer

Architectural base

AMERICAN MODERN

In 1925, a major international Modern design exposition entitled *Arts Décoratifs et Industriels Modernes*, opened to great fanfare in Paris. The United States was not represented in the show because the American design industry had little to exhibit that was truly Modern. Thousands of Americans came as tourists, however, and returned home with a taste for the abstract, geometric, cubist-inspired forms of the Modern style. In 1926, American enthusiasm for Modernism was further fueled by a traveling exhibition of some of the finest objects from the 1925 Paris Exposition.

Two factors helped win over the conservative American consumer to Modernism. One was America's longstanding love affair with technology and engineering. The other was immigration. By the late 1920s the list of foreign-born designers making significant contributions to the American-design landscape included such major figures as Paul T. Frankl, Eugene Schoen, Kem Weber, Walter von Nessen and Peter Mueller Monk.

With the rise of the Nazis in Germany in the 1930s, another wave of Europe's finest creative minds immigrated to the United States. Marcel Breuer, Lazlo Moholy Nagy, Anni Albers, Walter Gropius and Ludwig Mies van der Rohe were among the many European émigré designers who helped transform the art and design of their adopted country.

In the late 1920s, the skyscraper, that marvel of American engineering and architecture, had captured the imagination of the public. Paul Frankl produced his iconic skyscraper line of furniture, inspiring a host of designers to push the style even further and develop designs that celebrated the modern industrial world. Radical new materials—aluminum, chrome, glass, cork and various proto-plastics—were used in radical new ways. Reflecting America's love of technology and speed, designers began to create products with an aerodynamic look. Everything from high-styled furniture and sculpture to tableware, refrigerators, vacuum cleaners, even typewriters, were made to look as sleek and streamlined as the trains and planes of the period. It was the style that came to define the Machine Age.

Gilbert Rohde

PALDAO STORAGE UNIT,
c. 1938
The conical organic pulls on this imposing Herman Miller unit are hallmarks of Rohde's Paldao Group.
$1,500–$2,500

PALDAO EAST INDIAN LAUREL SIDEBOARD, *c.* 1938
This elegant Paldao sideboard features four concave doors with large conical pulls, interior drawers and shelves and flaring legs.
$3,000–$4,000

INSIDER'S INFORMATION

Gilbert Rohde was an important pioneer in the development of American Modern furniture design. His Paldao Group for the Herman Miller Company (named for the pieces' light paldao-wood veneer) was an important bridge between European Art Deco and American Modern.

PALDAO CHEST, *c.* 1935
A padded front distinguishes this Paldao Group chest.
$800–$1,200

PALDAO BEDROOM SUITE,
c. 1939
A magnificent ensemble by one of America's early Modern masters.
$8,000–$12,000 the set

Donald Deskey

DRESSERS, c. 1935

The sleek lines and sophisticated profiles of these Deskey dressers typify the elegance of American Art Deco.

$3,000–$4,000 each

BEDROOM SUITE, c. 1940

The aesthetic appeal of this bedroom suite derives from the chic interplay between black and white.

$3,000–$4,000 the suite

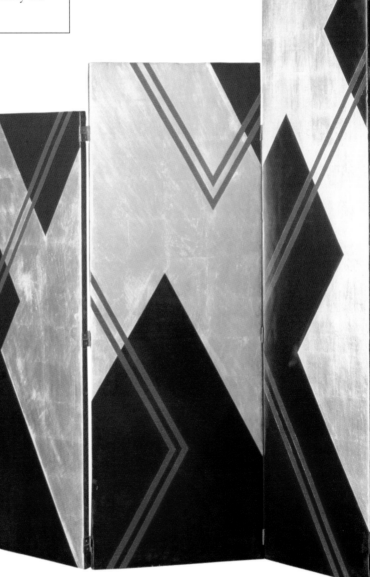

INSIDER'S INFORMATION

Donald Deskey's high-styled furniture defined the standard for American Deco. He was chosen to design many important public commissions—the interior of New York's Radio City Music Hall is probably his best-known work.

SCREEN, c. 1929

The glamour of Deskey's Radio City Music Hall interiors is evident in this dramatic wood-and-canvas screen by the American Art Deco master.

$40,000–$80,000

Heywood-Wakefield

CORNER CABINET, c. 1950
Typical of the Heywood-Wakefield Company's output, this practical corner cabinet was a great space saver in smaller postwar homes.
$1,200–$1,800

ENCORE KNEEHOLE DESK, c. 1955
Heywood-Wakefield's sleek and simple Encore line, introduced in 1949, was among its most successful productions.
$800–$1,000

ENCORE SIDE TABLE, c. 1955
$200–$300

ENCORE SIDEBOARD WITH CHINA CABINET, c. 1956

Heywood-Wakefield developed a wide range of furniture forms to meet the domestic needs of postwar America's growing middle class. This sideboard is available with or without the accompanying china cabinet.

$1,000–$1,500 the pair

WISHBONE CHAIRS, c. 1957

Wishbone chairs are the most popular of all Heywood-Wakefield's chair designs.

Chairs $800–$900 set of six
Table $600–$800

Eliel Saarinen

The Finnish-born architect Eliel Saarinen was a major influence on 20th-century American design, not only in his own right but through his groundbreaking program at the Cranbrook Academy of Art, in Michigan, where he mentored such postwar design luminaries as Charles and Ray Eames, Harry Bertoia, Florence Knoll, and his son, Eero. Having established himself as an architect and designer in Finland, Saarinen immigrated to the United States in 1922 with his wife, Loja, a textile designer, and young Eero. He went on to become the guiding force at Cranbrook and an innovative and prolific designer of buildings and furniture.

CRANBROOK DINING CHAIR, 1929

Saarinen's early designs in Finland were rooted in the simple yet elegant forms of Germany and Scandinavia. His subsequent American furniture and interiors developed this aesthetic further, often incorporating decorative influences from Paris or Vienna. Among his most outstanding work, and a high point of 20th-century design, is the furniture Saarinen designed for the Cranbrook Academy. This elegant light maplewood chair highlighted with vertical strips of black is part of the dining-room suite for the president's house at Cranbrook. The original 14 chairs are still at the school. Reproductions of these chairs licensed by Cranbrook and the Saarinen family retail for about $3,500 each.

BAR, c.1940

This mobile bar was custom designed by Saarinen in conjunction with fellow architect Robert Swanson. $3,000–$5,000

FLEXIBLE HOME ARRANGEMENTS BEDROOM SUITE, c. 1939

The Johnson Furniture Company of Grand Rapids, Michigan, produced several furniture lines by significant Modern designers, including Eliel Saarinen's Flexible Home Arrangements. $600–$1,200 each piece.

Warren McArthur

CHAIRS, c. 1930

Produced shortly after McArthur arrived in Los Angeles, these early pieces are more colorful and angular than later examples with the curving aluminum frames and "hockey puck" feet that became McArthur's signature.

Lounge and arm chairs
$8,000–$10,000 each
Loveseat $20,000–$25,000
Table $1,000–$2,000
Side chair $3,000–$4,000

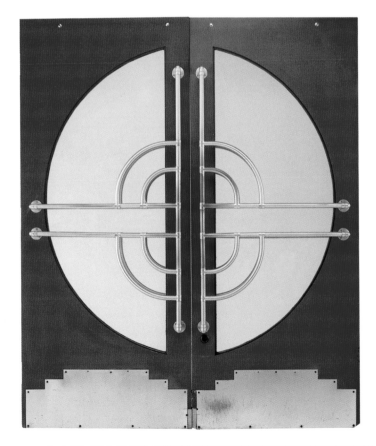

DESK AND CHAIR, C. 1936

The desk's curved-aluminum frame and "hockey puck" feet are hallmarks of McArthur's signature style.
$6,000–$8,000 the set

THEATER DOORS, c. 1940

These magnificent doors, with their curved-aluminum handles, epitomize the elegance and flamboyance of American Deco.
$3,000–$5,000

INSIDER'S INFORMATION

Trained as a mechanical engineer at Cornell in the first decade of the 20th century, Warren McArthur headed west after graduation to pursue a variety of careers. By 1929 he had made his way to Los Angeles, where he launched a metal-furniture business. His innovative tubular metal-furniture was immensely popular in 1930s Hollywood and remains highly prized by today's collectors.

Eugene Schoen

FURNITURE GROUPING,
c. 1934
Schoen's furniture and accessories are much admired today for their refined elegance, warmth and subtle use of color.
Screen $3,000–$4,000
Armchair $3,000–$4,000
Settee $3,000–$4,000

NICKEL-AND-GLASS CENTER TABLE, c. 1932

This sophisticated table was designed for the RKO Center Theater, in New York's Rockefeller Center, a smaller, more subdued neighbor of the flamboyant Radio City Music Hall.
$6,000–$9,000

CUSTOM-LACQUERED WOOD-AND-GLASS VANITY AND STOOL, c. 1937

Vanities tend not to be the most collected of furniture forms. Art Deco vanities, like this superb Schoen example, are the exception to the rule.
$8,000–$12,000

PAIR OF CUSTOM SCARLET-LACQUERED TWO-TIERED SIDE TABLES, c. 1937

Like most of Schoen's designs, these elegant side tables were executed by Schmieg & Kotzian, a partnership that brought fine Old World craftsmanship to America.
$3,000–$4,000 the pair

Paul Frankl

SKYSCRAPER CABINET, c. 1928
An icon of Modern American design. Its success led Frankl to name his company The Skyscraper Furniture Company.
$40,000–$80,000

ARMCHAIR, c. 1930
The original coral lacquer on this elegant Frankl armchair greatly adds to its value.
$5,000–$7,000

DINING-ROOM SUITE, _c._ 1935
The influence of the skyscraper is evident in the table pedestals and the vertical lines of the chairs.
$8,000–$12,000

DINING-ROOM SUITE, _c._ 1938
Frankl's designs for the Johnson Furniture Company incorporated innovative materials like the cork top on this dining-room table. Frankl's cork-topped furniture is a favorite of collectors.
$2,000–$4,000

American Chrome

WOLFGANG HOFFMAN CHROME-AND-GLASS TABLE, c. 1935

Hoffman's work for the Howell Company brought high style to chrome furniture. One of his most recognizable pieces, this round table commands unusually high prices for chrome.
$3,000–$4,000

GILBERT ROHDE SOFA SET, c. 1940

Rohde's chrome furniture is highly collectible today.
$3,000–$4,000

HOWELL DINETTE SET, c. 1940

This trim, compact leather-upholstered dinette set exemplifies the grace and style of mid-century chrome furniture.
$800–$1,200

T.H. Robsjohn-Gibbings

Terence Harold Robsjohn-Gibbings enjoyed a long and varied design career. Born in England in 1905, he was educated in London in architecture and interior design and his first job was with an English antiques dealer. He later worked for a film company producing interiors. In 1936, Robsjohn-Gibbings opened a showroom in New York, which he decorated with copies of ancient Greek statues and a mosaic floor. Like his New York showroom, his furniture designs reflected historical references and often a strong feel for ancient Greek lines and forms.

In 1943, Robsjohn-Gibbings started what would become a long and productive relationship with the Widdicomb Furniture Company of Grand Rapids, Michigan.

His impressive portfolio of designs for Widdicomb included dining room sets, couches, lounge chairs, coffee tables and bedroom suites, all in a conservative Modern idiom that incorporated organic curvilinear forms as well as pieces that relied on harder, sharper angles for their aesthetic punch. Robsjohn-Gibbings' relationship with Widdicomb came to an end in 1956. In 1960, he designed a line of classicizing furniture for the Greek company Saridis of Athens, and four years later he moved to Greece. The Saridis company still keeps in production Robsjohn-Gibbings' Klismos chair, his recreation of an ancient Greek design.

As appreciation for Modern furniture grows and becomes more mainstream, so does interest in Robsjohn-Gibbings' work. His well-made and affordable furniture is an excellent example of conservative, mass-marketed, mid-century Modernism. Especially popular with designers and collectors are Robsjohn-Gibbings' biomorphic coffee tables and brass-legged pieces.

SET OF NESTING OCCASIONAL TABLES FOR WIDDICOMB,
c. 1950
$1,200–$1,400

TWO LOUNGE CHAIRS AND OCCASIONAL TABLE, c. 1952
Table $600–$900
Chairs $800–$1,200 each

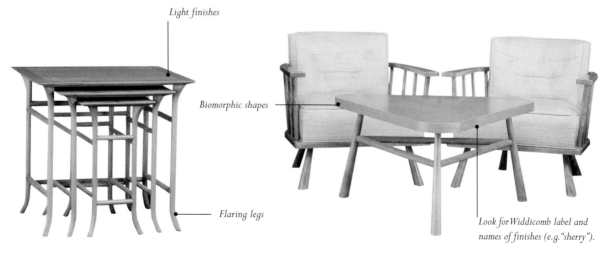

Light finishes

Biomorphic shapes

Flaring legs

Look for Widdicomb label and names of finishes (e.g. "sherry").

Eero Saarinen

Eero Saarinen was born in 1910 with design in his genes. His parents were the renowned Finnish architect, Eliel Saarinen, and textile designer Loja Saarinen. The family moved from Finland to the United States in 1923, where Eliel helped establish and became the first president of the Cranbrook Academy of Art in Bloomfield Hills, Michigan. After studying sculpture in Paris and architecture at Yale, the younger Saarinen taught at Cranbrook and joined his father's architectural firm in Michigan.

In collaboration with his Cranbrook colleague Charles Eames, Saarinen designed a line of furniture for a design competition sponsored by the Museum of Modern Art in New York in 1940. For more on the Organic Design in Home Furnishings competition, *see page 146*. Their molded-plywood shell Conversation chair won first prize in the living-room seating category, but the outbreak of World War II precluded its production. The prize-winning chair, however, served as inspiration for two of Saarinen's most famous postwar chair designs: the laminated plywood Grasshopper chair, manufactured by Knoll in 1947, and the 1949 Womb chair, his uniquely Modern interpretation of the traditional club chair.

Saarinen's greatest architectural project was the TWA terminal at New York's John F. Kennedy Airport. The building's highly sculptural, organic qualities were also evident in Saarinen's last furniture design, the famous 1957 Tulip Pedestal Group of chairs, tables and stools. In these "organically unified" pieces, a single plastic-coated aluminum pedestal supports either a tulip-shaped, fiberglass shell seat or a tabletop made of wood, laminate or marble. The tables were produced in various sizes, from small side tables to dining tables and large conference tables. An emblematic 1960s design, the Tulip Pedestal Group brought Eero Saarinen's brand of architectural Modernism into interiors across the country and achieved his goal of reducing the age-old visual clutter of multiple legs under tables and chairs.

**PEDESTAL GROUP
DINING SET, c. 1965**

Saarinen's famous marble-top table and six Tulip chairs.
Table $2,500–$3,500
Chairs $2,500–$3,500 for six

A SAARINEN KNOCK-OFF

Saarinen's Pedestal furniture was widely imitated during the 1960s. Though well-constructed, this table, made by the Burke Company of Dallas, Texas, is of distinctly lesser quality than a Saarinen original. In this Burke conference table, the top is Formica with a faux-wood grain. The tabletop edge is flat, whereas Saarinen's are beveled. The top is attached with large screws, while in a Saarinen table the leg screws into the top. Also, the legs do not taper gracefully as in a Saarinen table. In general, Burke pieces realize one-half to one-third the price of comparable Saarinen designs.

BURKE SAARINEN-STYLE TABLE, c. 1960
These pieces come in many sizes, ranging from small occasional tables to this large conference table.
$200–$400

WHITE-MARBLE PEDESTAL GROUP COFFEE TABLE, c. 1963
Saarinen used many materials for tabletops including white marble, shown here, teak, and formica.
$800–$1,200

Beveled edge.

WHAT TO LOOK FOR:

- ◆ tabletops with finely beveled edges
- ◆ knock-offs—many of these were made by the Burke Furniture Co. of Dallas, Texas

George Nakashima

George Nakashima's use of wood as an expressive aesthetic element is most evident in his tables. The large flat surfaces of Nakashima's Conoid-line tables were perfect showcases for the figured grain and swirling burls of his carefully chosen woods.

Tables were a major component of Nakashima's design inventory. He made several different models of small tables, coffee tables and dining tables. Some were supported by turned legs, others by trestles or by slabs of wood placed at right angles to each other. Each piece was made to order, so no two were exactly alike. With such a wide variety to choose from, it is important for the collector to understand the criteria used in valuing Nakashima's tables.

The character of the wood and the design of the table are the two main factors. A table top that has dramatic grain, intricate burling, openings, butterfly joints or an interesting shape makes a piece more valuable. Use of exotic woods also enhances value. Nakashima used American black walnut most often, but also worked with rosewood, laurel, elm, oak, cherry, and Persian walnut.

Furniture from the Conoid group made in the late 1950s and early 1960s almost always commands more than other Nakashima styles. The line's architectural bases and dramatic cantilevered effects make it very appealing to collectors.

Provenance is also an important factor in valuing a Nakashima piece. Examples from well-known commissions usually bring the most in the marketplace. Most Nakashima furniture is unsigned (usually he signed it only as a courtesy to clients who requested it). He did, however, keep extensive records that included wood type, furniture forms and dimensions. Those records from the years after 1954 were (and still are) kept under the name of the original buyer. If a collector knows the name of the original owner of a piece, its details and documentation can be verified, for a fee, at the Nakashima office in New Hope, Pennsylvania.

CONOID TABLE, c. 1966
The Conoid line is a great favorite among collectors, who are willing to pay a premium for these pieces. $20,000–$30,000

WHAT TO LOOK FOR:

- extreme burling
- figured wood, open areas in board
- cantilevered pieces from the Conoid line
- unusual woods

NAKASHIMA LOOK-ALIKES

Nakashima knock-offs abound in the market-place. The most reliable way to avoid buying a fake is to purchase only from reputable dealers and auction houses. Asking for a piece's provenance, or ownership history, is also a good way to check authenticity.

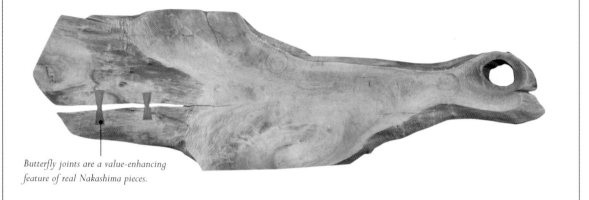

Butterfly joints are a value-enhancing feature of real Nakashima pieces.

MINGUREN COFFEE TABLE, c.1972

Unusual woods and highly organic shapes greatly enhance the value of this Nakashima table.
$15,000–$20,000

Openings and distinctive shapes usually bring more in the marketplace,

Isamu Noguchi

First and foremost a sculptor, Isamu Noguchi brought tremendous creativity to all his projects, from ceramics and lighting to furniture. Born in Los Angeles in 1904, Noguchi spent his early years in Japan and trained there as a cabinetmaker in 1917. He returned to the United States in 1918, and studied sculpture. He was awarded a Guggenheim Fellowship in 1927, which took him to France, where he studied with Constantin Brancusi. Returning to the U.S. again, he took up sculpting in New York in 1932, doing portrait busts to support himself. Among his famous clients was Martha Graham, for whom he designed stage sets for 30 years.

Probably the most easily recognized of Noguchi's furniture is his biomorphic glass-topped rose-wood coffee table, originally designed in 1939 for A. Congers Goodyear, who was the president of the Museum of Modern Art in New York. Variations of this table have been produced since 1944, beginning with the IN50 for Herman Miller.

Composed of two identical pieces of walnut locked together with a pin and socket, the base was held rigid by the weight of the glass top. Although the table's often imitated organic shape is taken for granted today, it was Noguchi who set the precedent for biomorphism with this truly innovative design.

In 1949, Herman Miller introduced Noguchi's Rudder table, with its biomorphic black-laminated birch top, a black finlike leg and two v-shaped wire legs. All of Noguchi's furniture designs display his love of form and interest in the relationship between the designed object and the space around it. His tables seem to float above the floor, rather than be anchored to it. A good example of this quality is the wire-base table produced by Knoll as a modification of his rocking stool. The metal-rod bases of these pieces suggest lightness and movement. The same feeling is evident in many of Noguchi's lighting designs, such as the Akari Group of paper lamps, inspired by Japanese lanterns and one of the most successful of Noguchi's commercial endeavors.

**ROCKING STOOL,
c. 1955**
Noguchi's tablelike rocking stools come in two sizes; both are extremely rare.
$6,000–$12,000

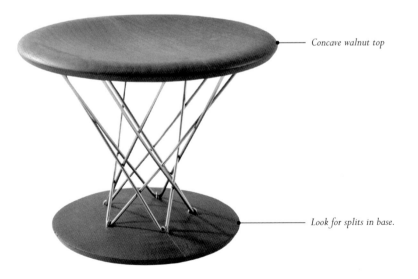

Concave walnut top

Look for splits in base.

WIRE-BASE OCCASIONAL TABLE FOR KNOLL, c. 1955

A fixture in corporate and institutional settings, this table is popular among today's collectors.
$1,600–$2,400

COFFEE TABLE, c. 1947

Produced by Noguchi for the Herman Miller Company, this icon of mid-century design has recently been brought back into production.
$800–$1,200

Older models tend to have green-tinted glass.

Contemporary tables have ½ inch (1.27 cm) glass tops. Vintage models have ¾ inch (2 cm) tops.

Richard Schultz

Richard Schultz's furniture lines are quickly becoming collector favorites. His Petal tables are especially well loved. They effectively capture the sense and feel of 1960s outdoor furniture design.

Schultz attended the Illinois Institute of Technology and joined the Knoll Company in 1951. At Knoll, Schultz helped Harry Bertoia develop his wire-chair line and participated in making other Knoll projects during the prolific 1950s.

In 1960 Schultz developed his own Petal Group, a family of tables designed to be marketed in conjunction with Bertoia's chairs. Schultz produced them in several sizes including a dining table, coffee table and occasional table. The tops came in several different finishes. Redwood is especially popular with collectors today. Knoll produced the tables until 1975.

In 1966, in response to a request from Florence Knoll, Schultz embarked on a project to provide Knoll clients with well-built, well-designed, architecturally sophisticated outdoor furniture. The result was the Schultz Leisure Group. This trendsetting collection of crisply Modern patio furniture offered the design-conscious consumer a sculptural alternative to picnic tables.

His next major design line was another variation on the outdoor theme. Working under his own label, Schultz developed and produced a line of imaginative furniture called Topiary. This group is made of aluminum perforated with organic cutouts that create a feeling of sunlight being filtered through a forest canopy. The Topiary series includes a lounge chair, bench, dining chair and chaise.

Schultz has recently and successfully reintroduced his most famous designs to a new generation that has embraced his vision as enthusiastically as their parents did.

SQUARE OUTDOOR DINING TABLE AND CHAIRS, 1966

Although designed for outdoor use, many people have taken Schultz's Leisure Group pieces indoors.
Table $400–$600
Chairs $200–$300 each

WHAT TO LOOK FOR:

- mesh seats
- aluminum supports
- redwood petals
- good condition

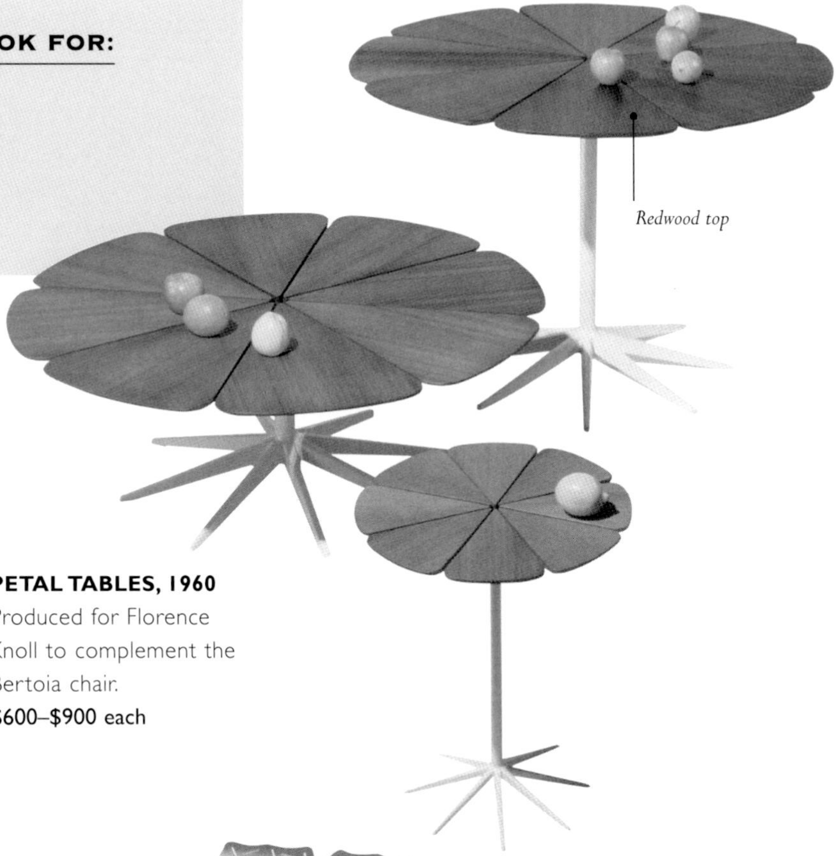

Redwood top

PETAL TABLES, 1960
Produced for Florence Knoll to complement the Bertoia chair.
$600–$900 each

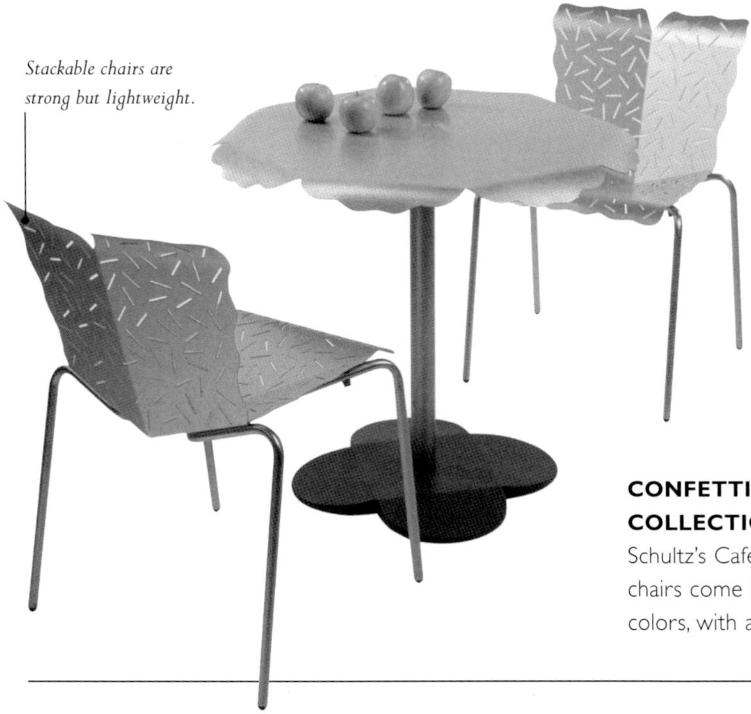

Stackable chairs are strong but lightweight.

CONFETTI CAFE COLLECTION c. 1995
Schultz's Café Collection chairs come in a variety of colors, with and without arms. The secondary market value of this relatively recent collection has yet to be established.

Paul Evans

Paul Evans was one of the most prolific and versatile artists of the mid-century studio furniture movement. His boldly dramatic designs incorporated highly unusual combinations of materials. In addition to introducing new welding and surfacing techniques and innovative paint and wash treatments, Evans pioneered the use of atomized bronze and aluminum, a sprayed-on surfacing technique that turned his bronze furniture into something more like functional sculpture.

Trained in sculpture and jewelry design, Evans began crafting art furniture in New Hope, Pennsylvania, in the mid-1950s. Throughout his career, coffee tables and cocktail tables were a very significant part of his total production. Evans sold his designs through his own studio in New Hope as well as through the national distribution network provided by his relationship with Directional Furniture Company.

The bases of Evans's first coffee/cocktail tables were made of looped screens commonly known as "fish scales." The tops of these tables were made either entirely of natural cleft slate or of slate trimmed with a walnut border. His next line of low tables was made of welded steel. In this series, large interconnected geometric shapes were transformed into table bases with crisp lines and sharp angles. The hard edges were softened by the addition of paint or chemical washes and fields of gold leafing. These tables were the first pieces Evans submitted to Directional for distribution through their show rooms, and they were a great success.

In the mid-1960s, Evans's Sculpted Bronze furniture was the rage among New York's avant garde. The Sculpted Bronze coffee and cocktail tables had tops of glass, slate and occasionally rosewood or walnut. Supporting these tops were radically shaped bases—cubes, arches, serpentines, and rings of stalagmites—that challenged conventional notions of furniture design.

Evans also made coffee and cocktail tables in Copper, Bronze, Pewter and Argente (welded

EVANS PE 240 STEEL DINING TABLE, c. 1968
A dramatic example of Evans's sculptural style.
$2,000–$3,000

Sculpted Steel base

aluminum). His Cityscape line of tables featured stylized skyscrapers as bases. Evans's New Hope studio remained an active distributor together with the Directional Furniture Company.

Collecting and decorating with Evans furniture is not for the faint of heart. Evans's work represents a rebellion against the tyranny of middle-class aesthetics. It takes a strong stand against the world of "sofa art" and matching upholstery. Decorate with Evans and you can bet the neighbors will talk.

WHAT TO LOOK FOR:

◆ natural cleft slate—Evans almost always used this grade of slate to provide his tabletops with subtle texture

◆ smoked patinas on steel surfaces

◆ welded signatures, gold leafing on exposed edges, bright colors and the integration of metal with organic materials such as wood or slate

Natural slate tops

Sculpted steel base

Gold-leafed edges

COFFEE TABLES, 1958–1965

A cross section of Evans coffee tables: an early ribbed example with natural-slate top (left); a sculpted steel example with a glass top (middle); a classic example of Evans's fish-scale style with a natural-slate top trimmed in walnut (right). $1,000–$2,500

DIRECTIONAL FURNITURE COMPANY

Directional Furniture Company of High Point, North Carolina was founded by Paul McCobb and V.G. Messberg. The importance of Evans's relationship with Directional cannot be overstated. It was a symbiotic connection that provided Directional with an inspired flow of cutting-edge studio furniture, while offering Evans unlimited access to the American marketplace. Thanks to his partnership with Directional, Evans's expensive furniture found a much larger market than it would have from his New Hope studio alone.

Gio Ponti

Steeped in the historical classicism of Italy, architect Gio Ponti sought the perfect balance between the past and the Modern ideal. Although born before the turn of the 20th century, Ponti's influence will be felt far into the 21st. His unique style is easily recognizable for the homage it pays to the classical, while always looking forward to the next innovation in technology and design.

As a writer, teacher, architect and designer, Ponti was a champion of Modern design in Italy. He began publishing the influential architecture and design magazine *Domus* in 1928, and edited it until his death in 1979. He served on the faculty of the Polytechnic in Milan, and was director of the Biennial Exhibitions of Decorative Arts in Milan, which became the showcase for Modern design after World War II. As design director of the ceramics firm of Richard-Ginori from 1923 until 1930, he produced the company's first catalog of Modern ceramics.

Italy's premier postwar architect, Ponti often designed buildings right down to drawer pulls and doorknobs. His prolific work included buildings, ceramics, furniture, glass, textiles and even appliances. The espresso machine he designed for La Pavoni in 1948 is considered a Modern icon, providing a bridge between prewar Bauhaus-influenced Modern and sleek postwar industrial Modern. He also designed glassware for Venini in the 1940s and 50s and the interiors of the ill-fated *Andrea Doria*.

His signature furniture design may well be the 1955 Superleggera chair, which provided a new perspective on traditional Italian country furniture. It is easily identifiable by its elegant tapering legs, ladder back and cane seat. Finely tapered legs are a feature of many other of Ponti's furniture designs, including his tables, and they give his work a wonderful sense of lightness. These pieces almost look like they are dancing on their toes. This is classic Ponti, and it is this light, stylized Modern aesthetic that makes his furniture both valuable and highly collectible.

LOUNGE CHAIR,
c. 1958

Ponti's designs encompassed everything from doorknobs, flatware and ceramics to furniture and buildings. This chair is a classic Ponti design sold through the Singer company.
Chair $1,200–$1,800

Ponti ceramic vessel.

Finely tapered legs are a Ponti hallmark.

WHAT TO LOOK FOR:

- sculptural qualities
- quality construction materials
- brass-capped feet

COFFEE TABLE, c. 1955
This elegant travertine-and-metal coffee table was distributed in the U.S. by M. Singer and Sons.
$2,500–$3,000

Travertine top

Metal base

Look for Singer label.

DINING-ROOM SET, c. 1960
This sleek set of walnut table and chairs combines excellent construction with clean modern lines.
$2,500–$3,5000 the set

Alvar Aalto

Alvar Aalto was born in Finland in 1898, a pivotal moment in the early history of Modern design. Aalto's architecture and interior designs incorporated the material integrity of the Arts and Crafts movement, the linear flow of Art Nouveau and the minimalist rigor of Modernism.

Trained as an architect in his native Finland, Aalto traveled extensively but remained firmly rooted in his homeland. As the architect of the Finnish pavilions at the Paris World Exposition in 1937 and the New York World's Fair in 1939, Aalto played a crucial role in bringing Finnish design to the world's attention.

At first, Aalto's furniture was usually designed as a part of a "unified interior," a concept popular with many architects at the time. In the late 1920s, Aalto worked with Otto Kornhonen to develop new methods of laminating and bending wood for chairs. The Paimio chair, designed in 1931 for a Finnish sanatorium, was a masterful application of cutting-edge form and technique to the organic

materials so integral to Scandinavian design. Aalto's look tended to be much "softer" than the designs of many of his contemporaries. His furniture had an inviting, comfortable feel that could be appreciated by the observer and the user alike. He also believed, as did other Scandinavian designers, that well-designed furniture could be inexpensive and widely accessible.

Often in collaboration with his wife, Aino, Aalto designed furniture, lighting, glass and textiles that his manufacturing firm, Artek, produced commercially at affordable prices. Aalto's furniture was practical, simple and beautifully made. Its quality and moderate price made it very popular in postwar America, and most of his original designs remain in production today.

One of Aalto's most interesting American commissions was designing tables for Harvard's Lamont Library. Recently deaccessioned, these tables, in good condition, are bringing over $10,000 at auction.

HARVARD LIBRARY TABLE, c. 1955

This bentwood table, produced for Harvard College's Lamont Library, is an excellent example of Aalto's minimalist style.
$10,000–$12,000

Look for splines in bend of legs.

Cast bronze feet

GLASS-TOP TABLE,
c. 1965
The Aalto hallmarks—simplicity, beauty and practicality—are all evident in this spare occasional table.
$1,200–$1,400

DINING ROOM SET,
c. 1939
An early example of Aalto's design, this set is still practical and stylish today.
$4,000–$5,000 the set

Wendell Castle

Sculptor, master woodworker, studio furniture visionary, Wendell Castle defies easy categorization. Born in Kansas in 1932, he trained as a designer and sculptor and received a Master's degree in sculpture from the University of Kansas. His early work was inspired by the studio master Wharton Esherick. Like Esherick, Castle relied heavily on organic naturalism to create an aesthetic impact.

Although Castle has worked with a wide variety of materials, even some considered radical or experimental, his abiding passion is wood. Much of his work can be viewed as part of an ongoing effort to fully understand and bring out the possibilities of this most varied and organic of materials.

In the late 1960s, Castle began to design fiberglass-coated plastic furniture. The plastic Molar chair has become one of his most recognizable and collectible productions. Inspired by Italian Pop, the lighthearted Molar chair, literally shaped like a molar, was produced by Castle's own company, Wendell Castle and Associates, and proved so popular that it gave rise to a Molar lounge chair,

child's chair, dining table and settee.

Starting in the 1980s and continuing on to the present, Wendell Castle embarked on a fantastic voyage through the excesses of Postmodernism. Using color, texture and shape, he created pieces that blurred the boundaries between sculpture and furniture. He made tables supported by arms instead of legs, buffets clad in sheets of verdigris copper, coatracks that bent and swayed as if in some strong wind. Castle's Postmodern work is amusing, charming, challenging, and instrumental in the redefining of studio furniture.

Prices for oustanding examples of Castle's work have been very strong at auction. His early organic and stacked laminate pieces often bring $20,000 to $50,000 for powerful examples. His Molar furniture and other plastic and fiberglass examples command between $1,000 to $5,000 depending on condition and form. His Postmodern work is still new to the market, but interest has been strong, and prices have hovered in the low five-figure range.

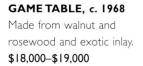

GAME TABLE, c. 1968
Made from walnut and rosewood and exotic inlay.
$18,000–$19,000

Fine organic design

PAGODA TABLE AND BUFFET, 1990
With rosewood veneer and turquoise-textured copper sheeting.
$14,000–$16,000

Rosewood veneer

CHERRY TABLES, 1990
Very unusual one- and two-tiered cherry tables topped by an organic chair sculpture.
$4,000–$6,000

WHAT TO LOOK FOR:

- exotic materials or stacked laminates
- a W.C. followed by a date—Castle signed and dated most of his work
- excellent construction techniques
- dynamic shapes, imaginative designs and extreme forms

FACT FILE
STORAGE

That human beings are not content to store their belongings in merely functional holders is evident from the decorative nature of storage pieces for at least the last millennium. Dressers, wardrobes, sideboards and credenzas have been made for as long as people have been accumulating possessions, but before the 20th century most people didn't own nearly as much as they do now. Early in the past century, families began to buy suites of bedroom furniture and cabinets that were meant to store the factory-produced clothing and objects that were becoming affordable for everyone. As access to goods increased, the need for storage created a vibrant new market for furniture designers.

The 20th century witnessed tremendous growth in the development of man-made materials such as plywood, laminates, plastics and metal plating. New materials and new production techniques were used to mass-produce furniture that was well-designed, well-made and affordable for the average person. In response to the rapidly changing, more mobile lifestyles of the 20th century, furniture became sleeker, lighter and more portable than it had ever been in the past.

This Fact File presents a group of furniture designers whose work displays a wide range of materials and forms. Jean Prouvé's brilliant use of industrial techniques and materials stands in contrast to the woodworking genius of Wharton Esherick and Phil Powell. Marcel Breuer's furniture for Bryn Mawr College was his first American commission. Florence Knoll's vision of clean lines and efficiency changed the look of the modern office. Paul McCobb's furniture brought good design to middle-class America, while T.H. Robsjohn-Gibbings gave high style to Modern cabinetry, and Piero Fornasetti added a surrealist patina to Italian Modernism. George Nakashima joined forces for a time with the Knoll and Widdicomb companies to make his passion for wood accessible to more people than he could ever reach from his own Pennsylvania studio. Vladimir Kagan also tried to bridge the gap between custom work and mass production. In addition to locomotives and cigarette packaging, Raymond Loewy designed plastic furniture. Paul Evans invented a metal composite that he applied to a whole line of furniture. The storage pieces highlighted in this section are a testament to the creativity and technological wizardry of 20th-century design.

Marcel Breuer

From his early experience with tubular steel to his pioneering work with plywood as a primary component in furniture construction, Marcel Breuer's contributions to Modern design are numerous and important. Breuer's career illustrates the broad nature of his genius and his laser-sharp vision of Modernism.

In 1935, Hungarian-born Breuer immigrated to England from Germany at the urging of his mentor, Walter Gropius. Political turmoil had diminished Breuer's commissions in Germany, and so he sought new opportunities in England. He found them at the Isokon Company in London, which manufactured designer Modern furniture. It was here that Breuer began working seriously with plywood. He designed five furniture pieces for Isokon, including his famous chaise longue.

In 1937, Breuer followed Gropius to America. He became Gropius' assistant at Harvard, but soon gained full professorship himself. Between 1937 and 1938, Breuer embarked on a commission for Bryn Mawr College—a prestigious women's school west of Philadelphia. He designed a five-piece bedroom suite for the Rhoads Hall dormitory. Included in the suite were a long rectangular mirror, a shelving unit, a bent plywood chair reminiscent of some of his earlier European work, a substantial chest of drawers with cut-in handles and an overhanging top and a dorm room desk that featured a large U–shaped support of bent plywood. This commission, believed to be Breuer's first furniture design in the United States, shows a logical design evolution from his work with Isokon.

In the summer of 1999 Bryn Mawr College deaccessioned Breuer's Rhoads Hall furniture. In a spectacular frenzy, pieces were snapped up and taken all over the world—a testament to the quality and popularity of Breuer's designs.

RHOADS HALL
SUITE, c. 1938
Chair $3,000–$5,000
Desk $3,000–$4,000
Chest $3,000–$4,000

WHAT TO LOOK FOR:

◆ case pieces signed Rhoads
◆ evidence of 60 years of college graffiti (some is pretty interesting!)

Jean Prouvé

France's Jean Prouvé was one of the most original designers and builders of the 20th century. When looking at his work today it is easy to forget how revolutionary it was when it was first produced. There was an intellectual purity to his geometric and functional designs that was stimulating and new. Incorporating early 20th-century breakthroughs in design, materials and production, Prouvé's work is not always easy to categorize or to appreciate for those attuned to mainstream aesthetics.

Born in 1901 to artist parents, Prouvé was trained in metalworking and was influenced by his father's crafts-oriented art collective, the School of Nancy. Prouvé opened his first workshop in Nancy in 1923, where he produced iron lighting fixtures as well as his first furniture designs. In 1930 he became one of the founding members of the Union of Modern Artists, and the following year he opened another design workshop, the *Ateliers Jean Prouvé*. His functional and socially-aware approach to architecture was evident in his public housing projects of the 1930s. In furniture design, he collaborated with Pierre Jeanneret and Charlotte Perriand, rejecting the steel-tube technique of the Bauhaus in favor of bent sheet metal. His functional, minimalist furniture was designed primarily for offices, schools and hospitals. As contradictory as it may sound, his work was machine-based craftsmanship that bridged the gap between art and industry.

Collectors have avidly sought out Prouvé's work, traveling all the way to Africa, in some cases, to find examples of his designs for Air France. As Prouvé produced far more furniture for commercial than for residential use, his scarce residential pieces sell at a premium. His storage units are readily adaptable to either home or office use, and for this reason they command significant prices at auction. The larger, more important of his storage units, such as the wood and metal Tunisie bookcases designed for the *Cité Université* in Paris, have sold for as much as $70,000 at auction.

WALL-HUNG CABINET, c. 1955

This Prouvé cabinet is equipped with sliding doors, making it ideal for use in a dining room.
$5,000–$10,000

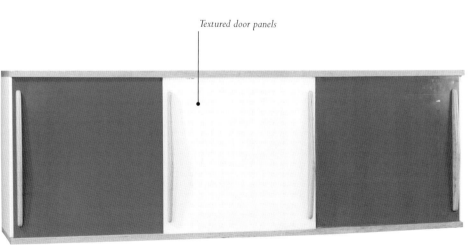

Textured door panels

ZIG-ZAG STORAGE UNIT, *c.* 1958

Small, sleek and space conscious, this is an excellent example of a Prouvé storage design.
$15,000–$20,000

Oak shelf　　*Breadboard ends*

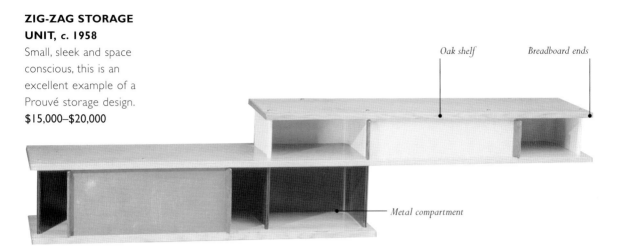

Metal compartment

WHAT TO LOOK FOR:

◆ metal mixed with wood
◆ primary colors
◆ protruding screw heads—a hallmark of Prouvé's furniture

WALL-HUNG STORAGE UNIT, *c.* 1956
$20,000–$25,000

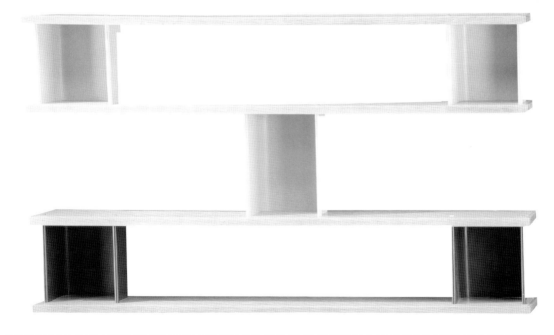

Florence Knoll

Florence Knoll's work was influenced by some of the greatest designers of her day. Walter Gropius, Mies van der Rohe and Marcel Breuer all had a part in her architectural education, and her designs reflect the European aesthetic. Her American interpretation of minimalist, rationalist design theories is clearly evident in Knoll's storage pieces. She mixed woods and metals to great effect and added laminates as they became popular. Dressers and desks are all spare in design but never lack for quality. Hanging cabinets have glass shelves, sliding doors and drop-down fronts that can be used as bars.

In the 1950s Florence Knoll's work was often displayed at the Museum of Modern Art's "Good Design" exhibits. Although Knoll did a great deal of residential work, the International Style she worked in was especially in successful corporate offices.

Knoll's vision for the "new" office was clean and uncluttered, and the corporate boom of the 1960s provided the perfect opportunity for her to change the way people looked at and worked in their offices. Her open-plan layouts created clean, uncluttered spaces—a perfect venue for her furniture. Companies like H.J. Heinz, CBS and Connecticut General Life Insurance all embraced this new way of organizing business space.

Knoll storage pieces are favored by collectors because many can easily make the transition from office to residential use. Because of their high quality, many have survived in excellent condition. Knoll's contract office furniture tends to bring less at auction than her residential pieces but the better credenzas can command between $3,000 and $4,000. Dressers are often good buys for entry level collectors, often selling for less than $1,000. Many Knoll office desks are too large for residential spaces and can be had for very reasonable prices.

WHAT TO LOOK FOR:

♦ identification tags or serial numbers on pieces—Knoll furniture was designed primarily for corporate offices

♦ blonde or rosewood credenzas and credenzas with marble tops—these tend to bring the most money in the marketplace

KNOLL DESK, c. 1960
An emblem of the clean, uncluttered 1960s corporate style.
$600–$900

Beveled edge

No pulls on drawers

Dowel legs

WALNUT-VENEERED CREDENZA, c. 1970

Florence Knoll credenzas made of teak or rosewood or that have marble tops command higher prices at auctions than this walnut-veneered piece.
$800–$1,200

Leather pull tabs

Locks detract from value

Square metal legs

WALNUT DRESSERS, c. 1968

With laminate tops and chrome pulls.
$600–$900

Formica laminate tops

Chrome pulls

Wharton Esherick

The artistry of Wharton Esherick successfully bridged the gulf between rural arts and crafts and sophisticated urban design. Born in Philadelphia in 1887, Esherick studied art at the Philadelphia School of Industrial Arts and the Pennsylvania Academy of Fine Art. He began his career painting and doing illustrations for local Philadelphia newspapers. In 1920 he converted his old barn into a painting and woodworking studio. In addition to creating powerful woodcut illustrations for books and other publications, he began to sculpt intricate designs in found furniture and to build his own unique furniture. It was his furniture more than his paintings that caught the eye of the local artistic elite. In 1924 Esherick completely abandoned fine art and committed himself to the creation of woodblocks and furniture. For the next 40 years he produced fine furniture, mostly on commission. He also designed and crafted entire interiors, often down to the smallest of details, like salad forks, cutting boards and light pulls.

Esherick furniture escapes easy categorization. He drew his inspiration from many different styles popular in the 1930s and 40s and yet had the ability to take the "design du jour" to its artistic limit. His boldness and creativity are evident in all of his furniture, from the early cubist examples to the later ornate pieces. Esherick turned his own house in Paoli, Pennsylvania, into a masterpiece of invention, using wood for every detail, from door latches to cabinets, floors and walls. The house is now the Wharton Esherick Museum, open to the public by appointment.

Esherick's work is very rare and enthusiastically sought after by collectors. Its scarcity makes his furniture quite valuable. Most freestanding pieces are signed and dated, but many cupboards and built-ins are not. Esherick's woodblocks are also of great interest to collectors and, like his furniture, bring hefty prices.

CORNER CABINET, 1951
This superb corner cabinet, a form found in Pennsylvania farmhouses, was crafted for a private commission.
$30,000–$40,000

BUILT-IN CLOSET,
c. 1951
A June Groff horse-motif
fabric covers the door.
$5,000–$8,000

WHAT TO LOOK FOR:

◆ a carved W.E. followed by the date—
Esherick often signed and dated his furniture

◆ simple oil finishes

◆ sensuous curves that invite touch

◆ unexposed surfaces or the inside of case
pieces painted in blue or salmon paint

◆ plywood carcasses

POPLAR CAPTAIN'S
BED, c. 1940
This simple, space-saving
design includes multiple
drawers in the headboard
and side rail and a poplar-
mounted metal lamp.
$20,000–$25,000

T.H. Robsjohn-Gibbings

Robsjohn-Gibbings had a great flair for the dramatic and often set standards and precedents for new looks in the design world. His pioneering use of bold colors in the 1940s was adopted in mainstream households years later, and his furniture was often copied. In 1962, Robsjohn-Gibbings and Edward Wormley received the Elsie de Wolfe Award for interior design.

Robsjohn-Gibbings never wavered in his devotion to classical furniture, Greek in particular. Yet in association with the Widdicomb Company of Grand Rapids, Michigan, between 1943 and 1956, he produced high-quality case goods with a true Modern feel. (Every so often, however, a saber leg inspired by the Greek Klismos chair would find its way into one of his Widdicomb designs.) Never a partisan of Bauhaus design tenets, Robsjohn-Gibbings was nonetheless able to deliver sophisticated, mainstream Modern furniture to an eager market.

Robsjohn-Gibbings borrowed freely from the elite world of architects and industrial designers, softening their cutting-edge forms for a clientele that was finally ready to let go of Early American furniture for something that would better reflect the character of mid 20th-century life. His furniture produced by Widdicomb was acquired by discriminating homeowners, both urban and suburban, throughout the United States.

Robsjohn-Gibbings's designs are distinctive and fairly easy to recognize. Prices for Widdicomb furniture are not as high as for the more cutting-edge designs of the same period, but because of its excellent construction and easy adaptability to various interiors, collectors have been buying Robsjohn-Gibbings furniture enthusiastically. The brass-legged pieces have realized the highest prices at auction, but there are good values to be had as Robsjohn-Gibbings finds his niche in the Modern market.

WHAT TO LOOK FOR:

◆ veneer chips along edges and bottoms, stains that have penetrated the wood and legs that are loose or wobbly—condition is very important when valuing Widdicomb furniture

STORAGE UNIT,
c. 1952
This is one of Robsjohn-Gibbings's seminal pieces.

Inside are dozens of cubby holes, shelves, and storage compartments.
$7,500–$8,500

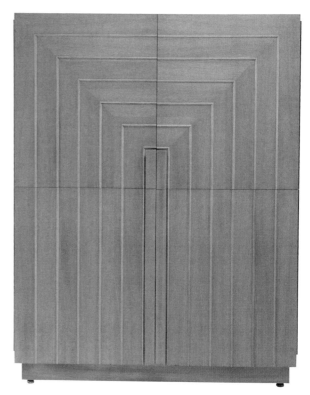

ROOM DIVIDER WITH DROP FRONT DESK, *c. 1955*

This spare, elegant yet highly functional pieces is a good example of the Robsjohn-Gibbings sophisticated urban design made available to the American consumer.

$2,000–$3,000

Examples with brass legs are usually of great interest to collectors.

BEDROOM SET, *c. 1950*

Bedroom sets were an important component of Robsjohn-Gibbings's design work for Widdicomb.

$1,400–$1,600

Look for Widdicomb labels with T.H. Robsjohn-Gibbings listed as designer.

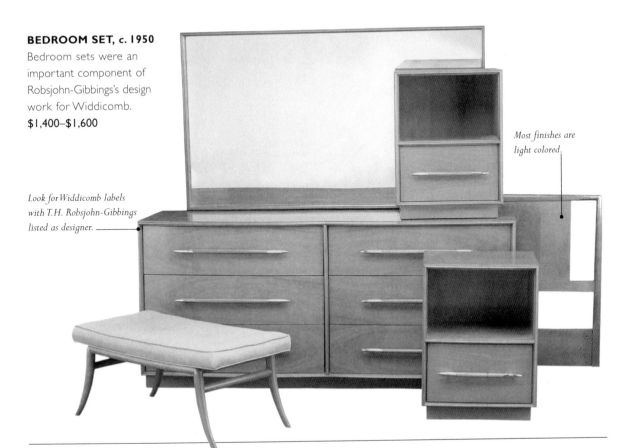

Most finishes are light colored.

Piero Fornasetti

Piero Fornasetti is an enigma in the world of Modern design. For the majority of Modernists, the primary goal of design was to reduce an object to its simplest state, stripping it of excess ornamentation and finding beauty and elegance in the object's basic form. This was not the case with Fornasetti, who celebrated ornamentation. He used decoration to overwhelm the sensory-starved Modern client. The trompe-l'oeil technique took a gentle jab at the stuffy and overbearing art establishment, much to the delight of the general art-buying public.

Fornastetti was born in Milan in 1913 and studied at the Brera Academy of Fine Arts. During the 1940s, Fornasetti was exiled to Switzerland with Gio Ponti. There the two began their long collaboration. In this creative alliance Ponti provided Modern forms for Fornasetti to decorate with his surrealist vision. It was an odd coupling of artistic talent. While Ponti designed furniture that was disciplined, spare and unapologetically faithful to the fundamental tenets of Modernism, Fornasetti reveled in the excesses of surrealism, relying on fantasy, illusion and a hint of metaphor to engage the viewer. Maybe it was this fundamental contradiction in styles that made the Ponti-Fornasetti collaboration so memorable.

Fornasetti was a prolific designer. During his career he produced furniture, umbrella stands, screens, dishes, ceramics and glass and, in 1984, a bicycle design. He manufactured and marketed his designs from his factory in his rambling Milan home. His son now carries on the business, reproducing his father's designs.

Fornasetti's designs have been prized by collectors for some time. As with so many Modernists, his work commands a wide range of values on the secondary market. Small objects that were produced in large quantities often sell for under $100, while some of his bigger case pieces can bring mid- to upper-five-figure prices.

TROMPE-L'OEIL UMBRELLA STAND, *c.* 1960

Fornasetti's decorative umbrella stands are relatively scarce and prized by collectors.
$1,400–$1,900

MINIATURE CABINET ON BALL FEET, *c.* 1960

This "palazzo" cabinet is another witty example of Fornasetti's trompe-l'oeil technique.
$1,400–$1,600

THE HERMAN MILLER COMPANY

The Modern furniture produced by the Herman Miller company of Zeeland, Michigan, defines innovation in 20th-century American design. The company's pioneering creative relationships with such mid-century masters as Gilbert Rohde, George Nelson, Charles and Ray Eames, Isamu Noguchi and Alexander Girard made it a world leader in progressive furniture production.

The Herman Miller company began in 1905 as the Star Furniture Company, a manufacturer of traditional-style bedroom sets. In 1909 D.J. DePree joined the firm as a clerk; that same year, it was renamed the Michigan Star Furniture Company. In 1923 DePree, in partnership with his father-in-law, Herman Miller, bought a controlling interest in the business and renamed it for Herman Miller, even though its namesake was never active in the company's operation.

A pivotal meeting in 1931 between DePree and the Modern designer Gilbert Rohde ushered in a new era for the Herman Miller Company. Rohde's sleek and sophisticated designs made use of such materials as Bakelite, Lucite, various metals, and exotic woods. By 1941 Herman Miller had ceased production of the traditional bedroom sets for which it had been known in order to concentrate on Rohde's Modern designs for storage units, modular desks, sectional sofas and electric clocks.

Gilbert Rohde died in 1944, at the age of 49. In 1946 DePree hired the brilliant George Nelson as his design director. In his new role Nelson had the vision to bring Charles and Ray Eames to the firm and to acquire the marketing and distribution rights to the Eameses' molded-plywood chairs and molded plastic-shell chairs. In 1947 Nelson established his own firm in New York City, which would provide Herman Miller with high-styled designs for home and office furniture and Howard Miller (Herman's son) with equally stylish designs for clocks.

That same year Isamu Noguchi developed his free-form, glass-topped table for the Miller firm. A year later, Herman Miller acquired the rights to manufacture and market Noguchi's biomorphic chess table. In addition to Rohde, Nelson, the Eameses and Noguchi, Herman Miller has had creative relationships with a host of important designers, including Alexander Girard, Don Chadwick, Ray Wilkes and Robert Probst.

The Eames-Saarinen Conversation Chair

INSIDER'S INFORMATION

In 1940 New York's Museum of Modern Art held a competition that would go down in history as a watershed in the evolution of 20th-century design. The "Organic Design in Home Furnishings" competition included among its jurors Alvar Aalto, Marcel Breuer, Edward Stone and Frank Parrish. First prize for living-room seating went to a pair of young designers who would themselves become 20th-century legends: Eero Saarinen and Charles Eames. Among their joint designs for the competition was the Conversation chair featured on this spread. Today, the extremely rare Eames-Saarinen chairs are among the most valuable pieces of Modern furniture in existence.

CONVERSATION CHAIR, c. 1940

In its use of molded plywood and cycle-welding to bond rubber to wood, the Eames-Saarinen chair represented a breakthrough in both design and technology. This version was produced by the Heywood-Wakefield Company in very limited numbers.
$80,000–$120,000

THE EAMES "LOOK"

Charles and Ray Eames are arguably the greatest husband-and-wife design team of the 20th century, perhaps of all time. Their creativity and passion for good design has had enormous impact on interior environments—both residential and commercial—the world over. The Eameses' influence extends beyond architecture and furniture design to encompass graphics, textiles, photography, film and even toys.

The Charles and Ray Eames design collaboration began shortly after their wedding in 1941. In their first California home, they continued the experimentation with molded plywood that had begun with Charles's collaboration with Eero Saarinen for the "Organic Design in Home Furnishings" competition in 1940. During the next six years, the Eameses developed some of their most timeless designs, including the LCW (Lounge Chair Wood), DCW (Dining Chair Wood), CTW (Coffee Table Wood) and FSW (Folding Screen Wood). Their creative synergy continued throughout the 1950s with such cutting-edge pieces as the ESU (Eames Storage Unit), Hang It All, the Sofa Compact, the Shell armchair on rockers and perhaps their most recognizable design, the 670 Lounge Chair.

Ray and Charles Eames experimented tirelessly with plywood, wire mesh, fiberglass and plastic resins, working first with the Molded Plywood Division of the Evans Products Company and later with the Herman Miller Company. The Eameses' work for both Evans and Herman Miller has been at the vanguard of 20th-century collecting. Their prototypes and experimental pieces have been the first examples of postwar design to break the six-figure barrier at auction.

SIDE CHAIRS, c. 1940
The Eames-Saarinen competition designs included these side chairs. Today such pieces are collected more as sculpture than as functional furniture.
$25,000–$40,000 each

Eames Chair: DCW/LCW

LCWS AND DCW IN FRONT OF AN EAMES SCREEN, c. 1950

The chair at left is an LCW, the rest are DCWs. Both lines are available in a variety of woods and finishes. (The Bubble lamps are by George Nelson.)

$400–$800 each

INSIDER'S INFORMATION

Among the most recognizable Eames designs are the DCWs and LCWs. Many factors contribute to their value. Red, rosewood, and slunkskin-covered models tend to be the most valuable, followed by birch and black analine dyed chairs; walnut and ash models bring the least. Examples with the Evans Company label bring more than those made by Herman Miller.

PROTOTYPE DCW WITH ARMS, c. 1945
Shown front and back, this armed DCW was handmade for exhibition at the Museum of Modern Art in New York.
$100,000–$125,000

"PONY" SKIN CHAIR, c. 1950
DCWs and LCWs covered in slunkskin are among the rarest versions of these chairs.
$10,000–$15,000

Nelson Storage

THIN EDGE BAR, c. 1958

Nelson's Thin Edge series comprised many different furniture forms, including this unusual bar.
$4,000–$6,000

THIN EDGE DRESSER, c. 1958

Thin Edge pieces with wooden legs are rare but do not bring as much as those with metal legs.
$4,000– $6,000

BASIC SERIES STORAGE UNIT, c. 1955

This version of the Basic series dresser features J pulls and hairpin legs.
$1,000–$1,500

THIN EDGE CABINET, c. 1955

Rosewood cabinets, like this one, from the Thin Edge series are highly sought after.
$2,000–$3,000

X-PULL CABINET, c. 1956

Nelson's Basic series allowed for a choice of components, finish, and hardware. X pulls were a popular option.
$1,000–$1,500

X-PULL STORAGE UNIT, c. 1956

This unit was designed to sit on top of Nelson benches.
$1,000–$1,500

Nelson Sofas

INSIDER'S INFORMATION

Although best known for his head-turning, eye-opening Marshmallow sofa, George Nelson also produced sofas in the classic Modernist idiom, with clean, simple lines that fit equally well in home and office. Their construction and materials were always of the highest quality.

MARSHMALLOW SOFA, c. 1957

This mid-20th-century icon was designed by Irving Harper, a key member of George Nelson's team. Fewer than 200 of them were produced between 1956 and 1965. The Herman Miller Company reissued the surprisingly comfortable Marshmallow in 1999, but original examples often command prices in excess of $10,000.

SLING SOFA, c. 1964
Although available in brown and black leather, Nelson's Sling sofa is more valuable in black.
$2,000–$3,000

SOFA WITH BUILT-IN END TABLES, c. 1958
Nelson often integrated storage units in his sofas and headboards.
$2,000–$3,000

Eames 670 and 671

INSIDER'S INFORMATION

A strong, masculine and comfortable 20th-century reinterpretation of a 19th-century English club chair, Charles and Ray Eames's 670 lounge chair and its accompanying 671 ottoman were the designers' first incursion into the high end of the furniture market. The comfort and quality of the 670 and 671 pieces ensured their initial success in the mid-1950s and their enduring popularity today. These collectors' favorites are still in production by the Herman Miller Company.

670 CHAIRS AND A 671 OTTOMAN IN FRONT OF AN EAMES SCREEN, c. 1958
The rosewood shells of these 670 and 671 pieces make them more valuable than comparable walnut items. An accompanying ottoman is also a value-adding factor.
670 chair $1,200–$1,800
670 chair and 671 ottoman $2,000–$3,000

EARLY 670/671 SET, c. 1960

The 670 chair and 671 ottoman were introduced in 1956. Although 670s and 671s with walnut shells are usually the least valuable, early examples like this set command a premium.

$3,000–$4,000 the set

TIGERWOOD 670 AND 671, c. 1974

This 670/671 set has tigerwood shells—an unusual, attractive and value-adding feature.

$3,000–$4,000 the set

Eames Storage Unit (ESU) Series

The desks and case units in
Ray and Charles Eameses'
ESU series are among their
most colorful and
architectonic designs.
Introduced in 1950, the
ESU series relied on
lightweight, off-the-shelf
materials to achieve the
Eameses' goal of low-cost,
high-quality design. Many
of these pieces have not
aged well, however, and
value is largely dependent
on condition and amount
of restoration. The
Herman Miller Company
originally produced two
series of ESUs. The earlier
series is easily identified by
its characteristic angle iron
feet. These first series
pieces are two to three
times as valuable as those
in the second series, with
their tubular feet. The
items in this spread are all
from the first series.

ESU 400, c. 1952
Its iconic status and colorful, flexible
and efficient design make the ESU
400 the Holy Grail of 20th-century
collectors. This particular example
in excellent condition brought
$70,000 at auction.

D10 SERIES ESU DESK, c. 1952
This boldly colored desk is back in production today. Original versions are valuable additions to any Modernist collection.
$5,000–$8,000

D20 SERIES ESU DESK,
c. 1950
Constructed of plywood, colored masonite and metal, this early hollowcore-top ESU desk has proven vulnerable to the passage of time. The value of such a piece depends in part on the amount of restoration it has undergone.
$5,000–$7,000

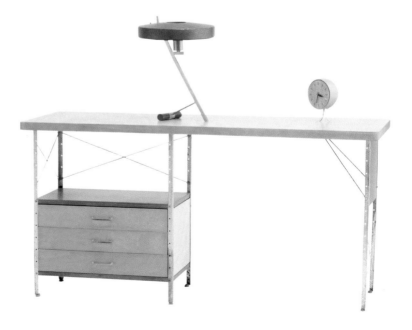

Nelson Desks

SWAG-LEG DESK, c. 1960
Nelson designed this compact, versatile desk for home use. Models with multicolor compartment panels, like this one, are more desirable than those with black-and-white panels.
$4,000–$6,000

DESK MODEL 4658, c. 1948
Simple but revolutionary, this Nelson desk includes a Pendaflex file drawer, a folding typewriter shelf and a suspended storage area above the writing surface.
$8,000–$12,000

Heywood-Wakefield

Many people who would like to collect Modern furniture face two immediate challenges. The first is geography. People living in urban areas originally purchased most mid-century designer furniture, and it is still found mostly in these areas. If you don't happen to live in New York, Chicago or Los Angeles, finding good examples of Modern furniture can be difficult. The second challenge can be cost. As more people become Modern enthusiasts, supply goes down and prices go up—simple economics.

Many collectors are finding their way around these barriers by collecting an American favorite—Heywood-Wakefield.

The Heywood-Wakefield Company of Gardner, Massachusetts, began its Modern experiment in 1931, with a line of furniture designed by Gilbert Rohde. This early Heywood-Wakefield furniture featured arching bentwood supports and bulbous modern lines. In addition to Gilbert Rohde, Heywood-Wakefield employed several other well-known designers, including Russel Wright, Count Alexis de Sarhnoffsky, Leo Jiranek and Alfonse Bach. The Heywood-Wakefield creative team produced a juggernaut of solid modern design at affordable prices, and sold it across America.

Heywood-Wakefield capitalized on the postwar recovery by introducing several lines of furniture that met with great success. Encore was a large, varied series of living room, dining room and bedroom furniture. The Sculptura and Riviera lines, made of blond wood with rounded edges, are highly prized by collectors today for their sophisticated postwar Modern look.

Collecting and decorating with Heywood-Wakefield can be fun and inexpensive. Most case pieces sell for under $1,000 and are usually available in most parts of America. There are a few exceptions. Room dividers, kneehole desks, roll top desks and exceptional examples of upholstered furniture can bring considerably more.

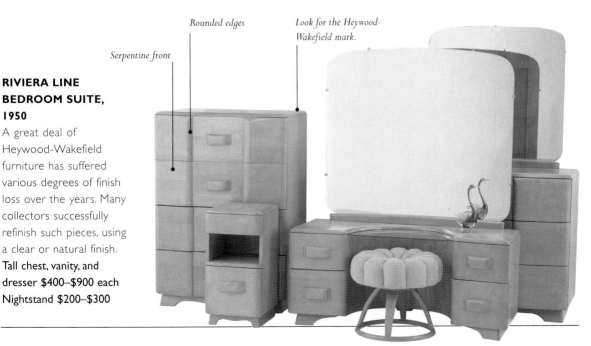

Serpentine front

Rounded edges

Look for the Heywood-Wakefield mark.

RIVIERA LINE BEDROOM SUITE, 1950

A great deal of Heywood-Wakefield furniture has suffered various degrees of finish loss over the years. Many collectors successfully refinish such pieces, using a clear or natural finish.

**Tall chest, vanity, and dresser $400–$900 each
Nightstand $200–$300**

George Nelson

After World War II, George Nelson reinvigorated the concept of personal storage to meet the aesthetic and practical needs of the modern world. Today, Nelson's case furniture is a staple of the Modern furniture trade, with three of his styles in particular attracting collector interest.

Designed in the late 1940s, Nelson's Basic Cabinet series included a wide variety of configurations. There were chests of drawers, with or without cabinets, some with wooden legs, others with metal hairpin legs, as well as chests set on benches. The series encompassed furniture forms designed to meet the entire spectrum of household functions, from chests, cabinets and vanities to radio and phonograph cases. All these pieces were available in a variety of finishes, from rosewood to lacquer (bittersweet red and black lacquer were especially popular), and with a choice of hardware. Pulls, for example, usually made of satin chrome, came in many different variations.

Nelson designed the Steel Frame group in the late 1950s as a less expensive alternative to the Basic Cabinet series, and it was often purchased for children's rooms. The chests, cabinets, desks, beds and nightstands in this line usually feature a black or white steel frame with multicolored masonite lacquered panels and elliptic metal handles.

The most sought after of Nelson's storage furniture is the Thin Edge group. It was, and remains, the most expensive of Nelson's storage lines, with rosewood-veneer being the most desirable finish, followed by teak. Most pieces feature slender chrome or aluminum legs; early examples have white porcelain pulls, later replaced by painted black or white metal or aluminum pulls.

All of Nelson's storage systems could be personalized by choosing a particular configuration and finish. Collectors today are constantly surprised to find such a wide range of forms.

ROSEWOOD THIN EDGE GROUP, c. 1956
Nelson's high-end storage line featured dramatic wood grains and fine construction details.
$3,000–$6,000 each

Porcelain pulls

Fine rosewood veneer

Most Thin Edge pieces featured chrome or aluminum legs. Wooden legs are rare.

BASIC CABINET SERIES, c. 1955

A mainstay of George Nelson's designs.
$1,500–$2,500 each

Herman Miller foil labels are often found in the top drawer.

Graduated doors on basic cabinet series

Wooden plank legs

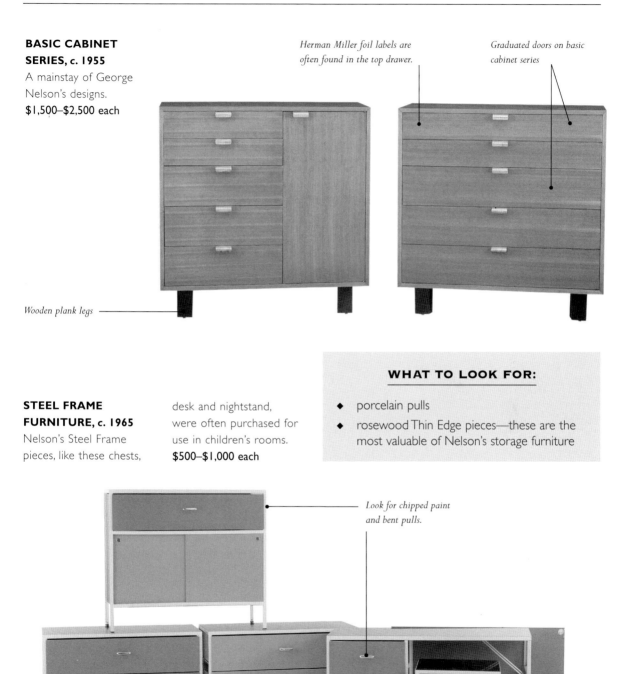

STEEL FRAME FURNITURE, c. 1965

Nelson's Steel Frame pieces, like these chests, desk and nightstand, were often purchased for use in children's rooms.
$500–$1,000 each

WHAT TO LOOK FOR:

- ◆ porcelain pulls
- ◆ rosewood Thin Edge pieces—these are the most valuable of Nelson's storage furniture

Look for chipped paint and bent pulls.

Paul Evans

Paul Evans's restless creativity found a perfect outlet in the production of storage furniture. He crafted cupboards and cabinets, buffets and disc bars. Storage units were the mainstay of his sales at both his New Hope studio and at the Directional showrooms. Like his tables (*see pages 122–123*), Evans's storage pieces are distinguished by bold combinations of materials and finishes.

Evans utilized all of his major techniques on his storage pieces. The two that come to the market most frequently and have the greatest collector following are Sculpted Steel and Sculpted Bronze. In his Sculpted Steel line, Evans organized multicolored sculptural elements into dramatic collages that were applied to the fronts of buffets, cabinets and other furniture forms, resulting in an explosion of color and texture.

Sculpted Bronze, the line most readily identified with Evans, was the fulfillment of a life's dream for him as he was now able to hand-sculpt individual pieces of furniture. This breakthrough brought Evans into the national spotlight, creating opportunities for him that were unimaginable to most studio furniture makers.

Many of Evans' storage pieces are wall-hung, adding both to their mystique and unconventional nature. Pieces that are not wall hung generally have plinth bases. Evans rarely used traditional leg supports.

Storage units are of great interest to collectors and with the exception of sculptures bring the highest prices in today's marketplace.

WHAT TO LOOK FOR:

- ◆ welded signature under doors
- ◆ piano hinges to support his heavy doors
- ◆ carcasses of case pieces covered with patchwork metal
- ◆ interiors painted in red or blue

WALL-HUNG DISC BAR, c. 1970
Made from sculpted bronze and distributed through Directional. Fewer than 200 of these were ever produced.
$4,000–$5,000

Sculpted bronze

Interior comprises a variety of storage options.

Large external hinges

SCULPTED FRONT
BUFFET, *c.* 1969
One of two known
to exist, this piece
exemplifies Evan's over-
the-top style.
$10,000–12,000

ARGENTE
WALL-HANGING
CUPBOARD, *c.* 1966
An exceptional piece in
an extremely rare style
for Evans.
$4,000–6,000

Slate top

*Date and signature
on bottom of door*

Phillip Lloyd Powell

Phil Powell's furniture often displays autobiographical elements. Nowhere is this more apparent than in his cabinets, cupboards, and buffets. Powell loved to travel and would often bring back architectural artifacts, small carvings, jewelry, chunks of colored glass and oil paintings, which he would integrate into his furniture, adding them to the swirl of his organic carvings. In one of his most extreme designs, Powell used Spratling silver bracelets as pulls on a wall-hung cupboard.

Powell's travels contributed more to his art than just a few trophies to add to his furniture. He gained inspiration and learned new woodworking techniques that became essential to his sculptural expression. In Great Britain, he learned how to apply gold leaf. Sicilian artisans taught him how to unleash the full power of wood by carving deeply into it. In Spain and Portugal Powell absorbed the contrasting textures and intricate patterns of ancient Moorish designs. Influenced by the beauty and mystery of Moroccan entryways, Powell made doors a prominent and dramatic element of his designs.

Probably more than any other studio furniture maker, Phil Powell personalized his work. Each piece is a travelogue of his amazing artistic journey.

Collector interest in Powell's work is on the rise, and so is its value. One problem that confronts the prospective collector of Powell furniture is the limited geographic range in which it is found. Always the purist, Powell shunned national marketing opportunities and instead sold most of his furniture from his New Hope, Pennsylvania, studio. His pieces are still found predominantly in the Philadelphia-New York City area, making collecting difficult for people in other parts of the country.

CARVED-FRONT WALL-HUNG CABINET, c. 1956

A great example of a Powell cabinet.
$4,500–$8,500

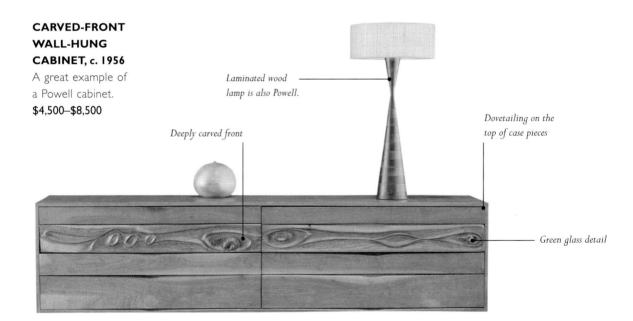

Laminated wood lamp is also Powell.

Deeply carved front

Dovetailing on the top of case pieces

Green glass detail

TWO-TIER STORAGE UNIT, c. 1957
This elegant mid-1950s cabinet features a pewter inlay.
$2,200–$3,500

Pewter inlay

Powell usually used walnut.

NAPOLEON AND JOSEPHINE WALL-HUNG CABINET, c. 1958
This very large piece came from Powell's personal collection.
$1,200–$2,500

Raymond Loewy

What do refrigerators, cigarette packs, elevator-operator uniforms, pencil sharpeners and the interior of the Skylab have in common? Raymond Loewy designed them all. Born in France in 1893, Loewy studied electrical engineering before he was called to serve in World War I. Immediately following the war he went to New York and landed jobs with Macy's and Sak's Fifth Avenue, where he designed those elevator-operator uniforms. He did illustrations and advertising for a number of fashion companies before moving on to industrial design. In 1934 his Hupmobile and Coldspot refrigerator for Sears drew public attention.

Loewy is considered one of the pioneers of Streamline design of the 1930s. The explosion of work that followed included china, textiles, trademarks (the Lucky Strike pack), interiors for passenger cars and the interior of the Skylab for NASA. All of this made Loewy one of the most prolific industrial designers of the 20th century. It would be hard to find an American alive during the 1940s and 50s who didn't have contact with Loewy's work in one way or another. The first mass-produced 35 mm camera, the Argus A, was his design. He also modified the Coke bottle, giving it the look that is recognized the world over.

Loewy explored the uses of every new postwar material in an amazing range of products. In the 1960s, as the use of plastics became widespread, Loewy designed a line of furniture that was manufactured by Doubinski Frères in Paris. It included dressers, cabinets, desks and credenzas made of acrylic, wood and metal. The design of this line, called DF2000 clearly reflected Lowey's commitment to an industrial aesthetic and the use of new materials and production techniques.

While there is interest in all of Loewy's designs, his DF furniture has drawn the attention of a wide range of collectors. These pieces are relatively uncommon and, in good condition command, strong prices.

WHITE LAMINATE DESK, c. 1966
This model features a sliding top over a tray with individual compartments.
$1,700–$2,500

Colors mixed in untraditional combinations add value.

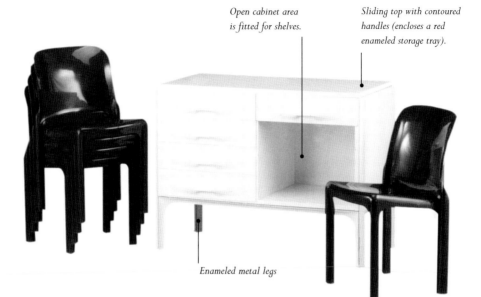

Open cabinet area is fitted for shelves.

Sliding top with contoured handles (encloses a red enameled storage tray).

Enameled metal legs

THE "STREAMLINE" LOOK

Loewy's influence on 20th-century design was pervasive, extending from the NASA Skylab to refrigerators, pencil sharpeners and the iconic Coca-Cola bottle. A particular fascination of his was the locomotive engine. He designed the one shown here, and his 1937 book, *The Locomotive: Its Esthetics* (London, The Studio), established him as one of the fathers of 20th-century Streamline style.

PLASTIC SLIDING-TOP CABINET, c. 1966

Loewy's high-end plastic cabinet is flanked by mass-produced plastic chairs of the same period.
Cabinet $1,200–$1,300

WHAT TO LOOK FOR:

♦ DF2000 series dressers, wardrobes and desks—because of its futuristic look and practical approach to storage, Loewy's furniture is eagerly sought after by collectors

♦ daring color combinations—these add value to any Loewy piece

Vladimir Kagan

Vladimir Kagan is one of America's most important contributors to mid-century studio design. From 1945 to the present he has turned out a steady stream of high-style, cutting-edge furniture.

His father, Illis Kagan, a master cabinetmaker and Bauhaus proponent, first inspired Kagan's career. The elder Kagan immigrated to the United States in 1938 and set up a woodworking shop in New York City. It was in his father's workshop that Kagan gained his first exposure to furniture design and construction.

While in high school, Kagan took classes from an architect who instilled in him a deep appreciation of architecture and the importance of integrating architecture with furniture design, of allowing form to follow function.

In 1947 Kagan was offered the opportunity to design the furniture for the first United Nations delegates' lounge in Lake Success, New York. Those early creations were not the highly stylized organic forms that Kagan came to develop later in his career, but instead were rectilinear with a more Bauhaus-inspired feel to them.

Another important experience in Kagan's early career was his collaboration with Raymond Loewy. For Loewy the young Kagan designed interiors and individual pieces of commercial furniture; he also helped Loewy with various aspects of boat design.

In 1950, through a chance encounter, Kagan met

BAR WITH TILE INLAY, c. 1950

This whimsical bar is an early example of Kagan's work.

$2,500–$3,000

Tile inlay

Plank-style legs are a hallmark of early Kagan.

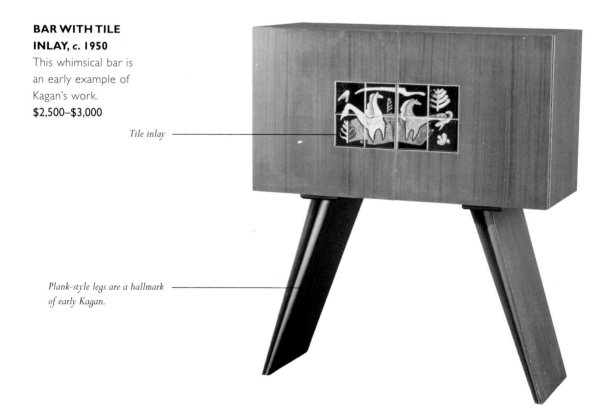

Hugo Dreyfuss, a Swiss textile designer. The two became friends and formed a partnership. From their store on 57th Street in New York, they sold Kagan's furniture and Dreyfuss's textiles to a who's who of important clients, including Marilyn Monroe, Walt Disney, Gary Cooper and the General Electric Company. By this time, Kagan's furniture had evolved into the sophisticated curvilinear forms with which he is most often associated.

In 1960 a recession ended the Kagan-Dreyfuss partnership. Kagan bought out Dreyfuss and closed the shop. Kagan quickly rebounded from this temporary setback. While his mid-century designs have become collector icons, he continues to create high-style Modern furniture for some of America's leading manufacturers.

WHAT TO LOOK FOR:

- curvilinear style pieces—these usually top the market
- Kagan's mid-century production—more recent pieces by High Point firms are untested in the secondary market

PARTNER'S DESK, c. 1968

This custom-made desk demonstrates Kagan's ability to provide a sleek form for any function. $6,000–$7,000

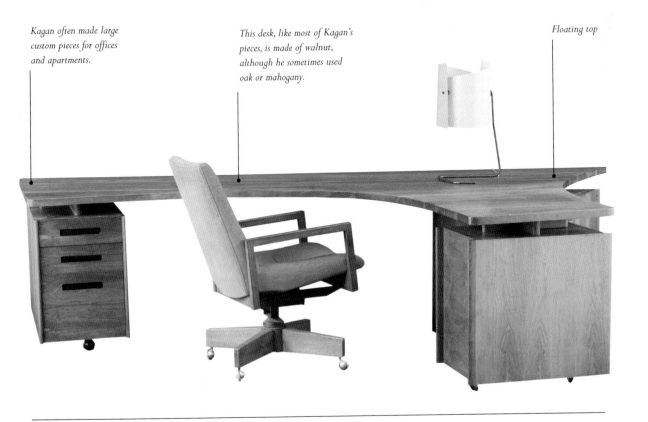

Kagan often made large custom pieces for offices and apartments.

This desk, like most of Kagan's pieces, is made of walnut, although he sometimes used oak or mahogany.

Floating top

LIGHTING AND CLOCKS

From the start of Modernism to the Postmodernists present, lighting and clocks have played an important role in communicating the Modern aesthetic. Every major design movement of the 20th century has reexamined lighting and clocks and left its imprint on them. From the New Hope, Pennsylvania, studios of George Nakashima, Paul Evans and Phil Powell to the corporate boardrooms of the Howard Miller and Lightolier companies, the era's greatest designers have concerned themselves with telling time and lighting environments. The Scandinavian Poul Henningsen designed lighting that helped to transform modern home and office interiors. Albert Cheuret and other French Art Deco designers lit up Jazz-Age interiors with their extravagant lamps and lighting fixtures, while in the United States, designers embraced the Machine Age, using industrial materials to produce sleek Modern forms that echoed the proud American skyline.

Many designers found their true creative voice in the production of clocks and lighting. George Nelson's postwar clocks, for example, are among his most inspired works. Wendell Castle redefined his own career and summed up the entire Postmodern movement through his clocks. The era of industrial design in the United States is encapsulated in the lighting it produced.

As in every collecting field, rarity and desirability determine the value of Modern clocks and lighting. Because some well-designed clocks and lamps were made in large numbers, they remain affordable; others were produced in limited quantities and are very expensive. Prices cover such a wide range that there is something for everyone in this market.

Albert Cheuret's clocks and chandeliers can bring upward of $100,000. Prototypes of clocks produced by the Howard Miller Company of Zeeland, Michigan, have sold for $10,000 to $20,000. Heifetz lamps, expensive when first produced, can command $1,000 to $10,000 today, depending on the model. In contrast, George Nelson Bubble lamps were widely available and affordable when new and sell today for no more than a few hundred dollars each. Well-designed clocks and lighting by anonymous designers can often be acquired at low cost. In fact, this is one area of Modern collecting in which a great example without a known pedigree can still inspire collector interest.

Secessionist Lamps

The Vienna Secessionist movement began in 1897 as a reaction against the established and accepted art of the academy. Its founding members believed Art Nouveau to be extravagant to the point of decadence and told the world so in their journal *Sacred Spring*, first published in 1898.

The Wiener Werkstätte was a Viennese arts and crafts cooperative that rejected the industrialization and mechanization of artistic expression. Like the Arts and Crafts movement in England and America, the Wiener Werkstätte believed that objects for the home should be beautifully crafted and produced by hand. Members of the workshop also believed in the direct connection between craftsperson and purchaser. Public access to their output, however, was limited because these one-of-a-kind items were labor intensive and costly to produce.

Working in a traditional guild environment that allowed the free flow of ideas, the Secessionists created an extraordinary array of furniture, ceramics, lamps and other decorative arts.

The ceramics of the Secessionists include an extremely broad range of styles, from Michael Powolny's puttis and curlicues to Vally Wieselthier's colorful geometric terra-cotta heads and lamp bases and Susi Singer's witty stoneware. The workshop's women designers were especially influential in shaping 1920s Austrian design. Inspiration was drawn from all over the globe—Japanese and Egyptian art, Cubism, indigenous and primitive art and Futurist elements were combined in fresh surprising ways. No fine European interior of the 1920s was complete without a lamp, ashtray, box or figurine from the Wiener Werkstätte.

Viennese lighting is available in a wide range of forms, from rare and costly Moser chandeliers to whimsical, colorful ceramic lamps. Most pieces are carefully marked, and artists whose work is in great demand by collectors command the highest prices, provided an object is in excellent condition. Terra-cotta items are not as durable as porcelain and stoneware and often exhibit flaking and chipping.

VALLY WIESELTHIER LAMP BASE, c. 1920
An intricate example of Secessionist ceramic ware.
$1,000–$1,500

Look for "WW" (Wiener Werkstätte) and artist's monogram on the bottom.

KITTY RIX DOUBLE-HANDLED LAMP BASE, c. 1920
Rix was a leading ceramic artist at the Wiener Werkstätte.
$1,000–$1,500

Asymmetrical handles

Red clay bodies chip easily at bases.

Gilbert Rohde Clocks

Gilbert Rohde's large body of work provided a bridge between Art Deco and Modernism. Born in New York in 1884, Rohde studied art and worked as an illustrator as well as in photography and journalism before trying his hand at furniture design. The Modern furniture he saw on a trip to France and Germany in 1927 heavily influenced him. In 1929 he opened a studio in New York. Between 1930 and 1931 he designed two lines of furniture for Heywood-Wakefield of Gardner, Massachusetts. Rohde also did work for Troy Sunshade (the Z chair and stool), Widdicomb and Thonet. The popularity of his designs during the difficult Depression era is testimony to his creativity and resourcefulness.

Rohde began a very successful collaboration with Herman Miller in 1931. His work for Miller's clock subsidiary, the Herman Miller Clock Company, provides a good insight into the transition from Deco to Modern design. Art Deco-style numerals give way to balls as placeholders. The Z clock even did away with the traditional clock case while its face incorporated the most up-to-date materials, including pearl celluloid and Formica. The company went bankrupt in the late 1930s, but not before Rohde had made a permanent impression on clock design.

He went on to serve on the design committee for the 1939 New York World's Fair and was the head of industrial design for the School of Architecture at New York University between 1939 and 1943.

There has been a surge of interest in Rohde's clocks. As the homes of Modern furniture collectors fill up with case goods, the popularity of Modern accessories grows! Prices range from $1,000 to $9,000 for rare examples in good condition.

ELECTRIC DESK CLOCK #4083, c. 1940
$2,500–$3,500

WHAT TO LOOK FOR:

- condition—this is extremely critical in evaluating Rohde clocks
- original hands, especially second hands, and original electric cords—both add to value
- functional—clocks should work and keep reasonable time to bring optimum price
- Herman Miller labels, as there is no singular configuration that readily identifies Rohde clocks

Z CLOCK,
c. 1938
This Rohde design was one of the first attempts to apply modern design to clocks.
$5,000–$8,000

WORLD'S FAIR CLOCK, c. 1939
This is another early example of Rohde's Modern clock designs.
$2,000–$5,000

Art Deco Lighting

The breadth of ingenuity and creativity in Art Deco lighting is evident to anyone who collects it. In the 1920s the definition of Modernism was not yet set in stone, new industrial technologies were developing at a rapid pace and the range of new materials available to designers was growing exponentially. These conditions were the incubator for the innovative designs of the Art Deco period. Informed by the tenets of European minimalism and a desire for form to follow function, Art Deco gave rise to dozens of different designers eager to try their hand at lighting design.

These bold spirits experimented and pushed the limits of technology, materials and the very concept of the lamp. In Europe, Le Chevallier, Chareau, Cheuret, Dunand, Herbst, Adnet and Gray, among others, all developed highly creative, novel approaches to lighting.

Across the Atlantic, von Nessen, Rohde, Deskey, Teague and others replaced the highly ornate lamps of the Art Nouveau period with designs that were opulent and dramtic but cast in a more Modern idiom. The American designers reinterpreted French Deco and the result was an American Deco style that was distinctive and fresh.

The dramatic nature of Art Deco lighting has always attracted a large following of dedicated collectors. Deco lighting offers the enthusiast a wide range of collecting possibilities. Rare, unusual or one-of-a-kind designs by the French Deco masters often bring phenomenal prices. Albert Cheuret lighting, for example, regularly commands prices over $30,000. Eileen Gray's designs can bring even stronger prices.

Well-designed but unattributed Deco lamps can be good value, but it is the lamps attributed to well-known designers that are in greatest demand. Among the Americans whose lamps bring a premium are Donald Deskey, Gilbert Rohde and Arthur Darwin Teague. While American lamps have not realized the prices of European lighting, many regularly sell in the $5,000 to $10,000 range.

CHEURET LIGHTING FIXTURE, c. 1935
The value of Cheuret's bird-motive alabaster and bronze chandelier depends on its condition. This example would be worth considerably more ($60,000–$70,000) with its original alabaster.
$35,000–$45,000

PAIR OF LALIQUE GRAND DEPOT LAMPS, c. 1928

René Lalique's Art Deco glass creations ranged from lamps and clocks to perfume bottles and hood ornaments.

CHEURET TULIP LAMP, c. 1925

A graceful silvered-bronze and alabaster Cheuret design.
$8,000–$10,000

PAIR OF EDGAR BRANDT LAMPS, c. 1930

These classic Art Deco wrought-and-polished-metal lamps feature alabaster shades.
$8,000–$10,000 the pair

Postwar Lighting

Postwar lighting is one of the most interesting collecting areas for aficionados of Modern design. A common complaint among collectors is that value is often based on attribution to one of a relatively small number of "name" designers. Although this is true of most areas of Modernism, lighting is an exception to the rule. Good lighting design is often appreciated regardless of its "name brand."

The extraordinary range of good Modern lamps and lighting fixtures encompasses everything from colorful Italian pottery lamps produced by Raymor to the sleek, sophisticated lighting designs created by Heifitz.

Great lighting can be found in every major design movement. Scandinavian Modern boasts Paavo Tynell's innovative lamps, as well as the creations of Artek and Atelje Lyktan. Italian Modern lamps by such companies as Stilnovo, Artemide and Fontana Arte are distinguished by their strong forms and fine quality. Japan, Great Britain, France and West Germany produced many fine lighting manufacturers, while American lighting is well-represented by such firms as Laurel and Lightolier.

Look for high-quality construction and materials and unusual forms. Lighting is one of the few design arenas in which the amusing and clever are acceptable and indeed often desirable. Furniture is a more serious business, and good examples of interesting stylish lighting can add interest to interiors and "lighten up" serious collections.

The range of lamp prices is very broad. Remarkably, some of the most heated bidding in many auctions erupts when a really great lamp comes through, whether marked or not. Replaced cloth shades rarely affect value, but replacing glass or metal shades usually reduces it significantly. Rewiring also has little to no impact on overall value.

RAYMOR FLOOR RANGE, c. 1955
The Raymor Company imported dozens of cutting-edge lighting design, like this one, during the 1950s.
$2,000–$3,000

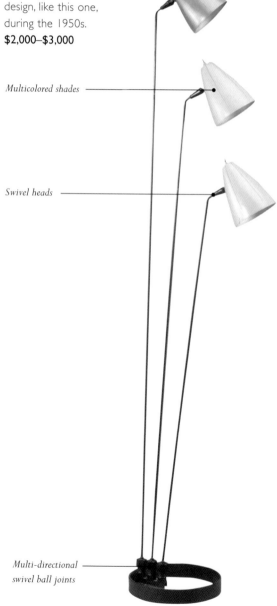

Multicolored shades

Swivel heads

Multi-directional swivel ball joints

WALL-MOUNTED METAL LIGHT FIXTURE, c. 1955

Unconstrained by convention, mid-century lighting designers broadened the horizons of their field. This unidentified fixture illustrates the fact that, unlike Modern furniture, Modern lighting does not require a pedigree to realize significant prices in the marketplace.

$400–$600

LAUREL LAMP, c. 1960

This classic 1960s lighting design comes in a variety of colors and sizes.

$400–$600

LIGHTOLIER DESK LAMP, c. 1955

The architectural form of this Lightolier lamp is rare and very striking.

$600–$900

Shade is not connected to base. Be careful when handling.

George Nelson Clocks

After graduating as an architect from Yale University in 1931, George Nelson did not limit his interests to buildings. He edited design and architectural magazines and was a noted writer and lecturer. Between 1946 and 1965, he served as the design director for Herman Miller. His accomplishments in Modern design and manufacture are legendary, and his associations with the most important designers of the 20th century produced a large percentage of what is now considered classic modern.

Nelson was a great proponent of open-space living, and the spareness and utility of his furniture for home and office, as well as his line of clocks, reflected his credo.

Nelson designed clocks for the Howard Miller Clock Company in Zeeland, Michigan. (Howard was Herman's son.) His first design was the 1949 Atomic or Ball wall clock. Inspired by the atom's structure, this 1950s icon reflects the era's fascination with things atomic. Designed over the course of 30-plus years, Nelson's Chronopak series included table and wall clocks in a variety of styles. Many designs feature rays or spokes that radiate from a central cylinder, with hands that seem to float against their backgrounds. The most sought after of Nelson's clocks are prototypes and limited production models.

Collecting Modern clocks has become popular, and prices have escalated as the competition intensifies for the rarest examples of Nelson's clocks. Space-conscious collectors find these clocks easy to fit into even the smallest apartments, and their bold colors and arresting designs make them dramatic additions to any Modern collection.

The range of values for Nelson clocks is broad. Prototypes have brought as much as $12,000, while some lesser models bring only $200 to $300. The best examples, as expected, have original parts and are in working condition.

**KITE TABLE CLOCK,
c. 1957**
Fine and rare George Nelson for Howard Miller prototype Kite table clock, with a diamond-shaped face enameled in yellow and khaki and black bead hour markers on ivory-enameled metal pins. (From the collection of a Nelson associate designer). $12,000–$18,000

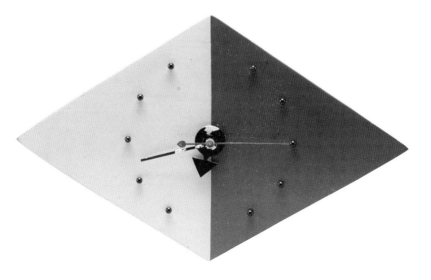

SPIDERWEB WALL CLOCK c. 1958
This dramatic clock features a wood center, enameled metal rays, and black string. The Howard Miller label on the back is black.
$1,000–$1,500

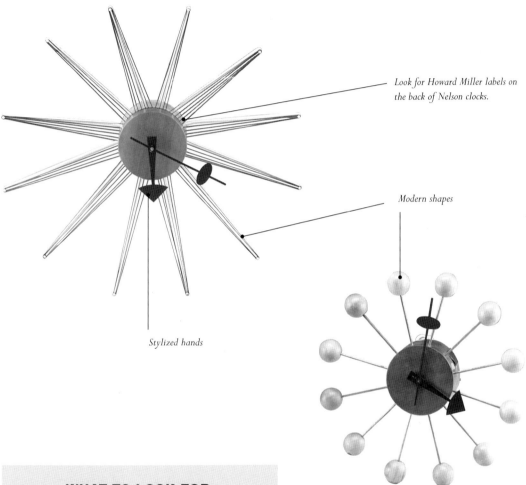

Look for Howard Miller labels on the back of Nelson clocks.

Modern shapes

Stylized hands

WHAT TO LOOK FOR:

◆ general condition—a very important factor in valuing Nelson clocks
◆ intact second hands
◆ original paint
◆ good working condition

BALL CLOCK, c. 1955
On this example of Nelson's iconic Ball or Atomic clock, walnut hour markers radiate from a brass center with black enameled hands. The Howard Miller label on the back is gold.
$400–$600

George Nelson Lamps

George Nelson was an excellent choice to follow Gilbert Rohde as director of design for Herman Miller in 1946. His tenure lasted until 1965, and during this 20-year span, Nelson and his associates produced a large and important body of work.

A good deal of Nelson's output was produced in collaboration with others. His Bubble lamp was actually designed with William Renwick, although it is normally credited to Nelson. The Howard Miller Clock Company manufactured the collection of lamps between 1947 and 1952. These lamps were made of translucent plastic material sprayed over a metal frame. As their basic design allowed for many different sizes and shapes, there are dozens of variations on the Bubble theme. Collectors are especially fond of unusual shapes—round Bubble lamps are the most common. Floor and table models are especially desirable, but they are hard to find. The Half Nelson table lamp was also produced through Howard Miller but only for a short time. Condition is especially important in these lamps as many have been discolored by nicotine and are not cleanable. Small holes are common and significantly reduce value.

Rare and unusual Bubble lamps command over $1,500, while the typical round model brings only between $150 and $200 because it is so common.

In addition to clocks and lamps, Nelson Associates designed birdhouses, weathervanes and garden pottery also manufactured by Howard Miller in small numbers. These items are rarely found in the marketplace, and steep competition for them drives up prices.

SET OF FOUR NELSON BUBBLE LAMPS, c. 1950
In the realm of Bubble lamps, the more interesting and unusual the shape, the greater its appeal.
$300–$400 each

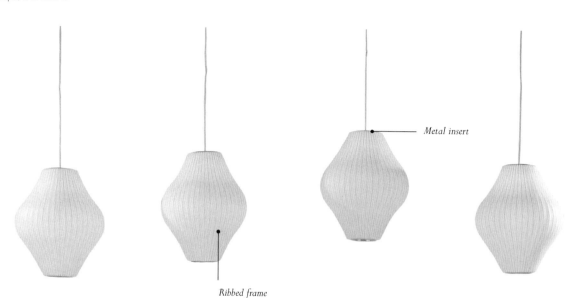

Metal insert

Ribbed frame

WHAT TO LOOK FOR:

♦ condition—a critical factor in valuing Bubble lamps

♦ yellowing caused by smoking—significantly reduces value

♦ holes and tears—these defects can make Bubble lamps worthless; make sure to inspect them carefully before purchase

PROTOTYPE NELSON LAMP, c. 1957

This rare and valuable prototype was designed to complement the Bubble lamp series.
$2,500–$3,000

BUBBLE LAMP, c. 1960

A pleasing addition to any interior, Bubble lamps are both stylish and practical.
$300–$500

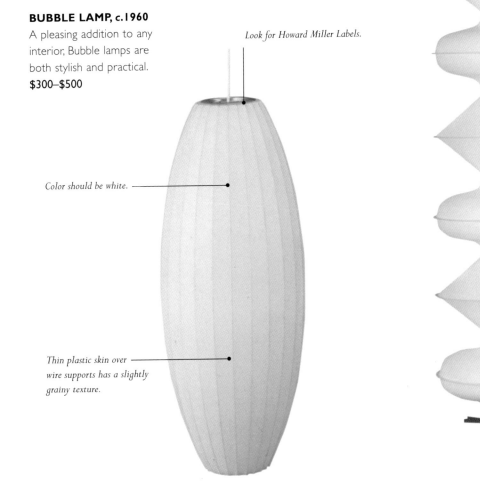

Look for Howard Miller Labels.

Color should be white.

Thin plastic skin over wire supports has a slightly grainy texture.

Hard plastic

Studio Lighting

The loosely defined concept of studio furniture has always encompassed several other areas of creative interior design, most notably lighting. Most of the studio masters designed lamps and lighting fixtures to accompany their hand-crafted furniture or as favors to important clients and, in some instances, as part of complete interior-design commissions.

Phil Powell began his career designing lamps in a distinctively Modern style. These early pieces were constructed from wood given to him by George Nakashima. Powell continued to produce lighting designs throughout his career.

Lighting was a major component of Paul Evans's overall design inventory. His welded steel pole lamp was one of his first commercially successful designs.

George Nakashima's Kent Hall Lamp is a Modern icon. Designed in 1964 for a building at Columbia University, it brings strong prices at auction, as does other lighting by Nakashima.

Wharton Esherick is another of Eastern Pennsylvania's favorite design sons. His lighting designs were closely integrated with his interiors. In his house and studio, now a public museum, Esherick demonstrated complete mastery of all interior details from lamps and lighting fixtures to the decorated switch plates.

Smokey Tunis, a mysterious studio furniture maker and artist, designed and crafted wild folk-art style furniture in Westchester County, New York. Unfortunately, like so many other studio artists, little is known about Smokey Tunis. He might have been lost to history had his work not been discovered by a small group of collectors.

Studio lighting has always been a popular item to collect, thanks to its good design, superb craftsmanship and strong individuality.

SMOKEY TUNIS LAMP, c. 1956

Does it get more over the top than this? The body is a wooden frame covered in a multicolored gesso, and is signed "Tunis" at the bottom. Smokey Tunis's work is very rare and collected by a small group of enthusiastic collectors, including several well known entertainers.

$4,000–$6,000

Painted glass shade

Gesso-covered wood frame

Tunis signature

◆ signed pieces—many examples of studio lighting are not signed so provenance becomes important

WALNUT SUPPORT — *Walnut support*

Parchment

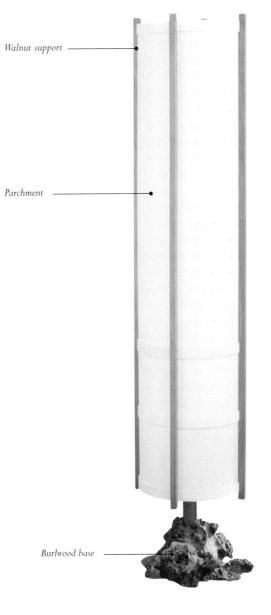

WHARTON ESHERICK TABLE LAMP, 1931

A dramatically sculptural walnut table lamp by the Pennsylvania master.
$6,000–$9,000

Burlwood base

Look for "WE" signature and date on Esherick pieces.

GEORGE NAKASHIMA KENT HALL LAMP, 1964

This version of the 5-feet (1.5-m) tall Kent Hall Lamp is exceedingly rare and brings high prices at auction.
$12,000–$18,000

Arteluce Lamps

What the Herman Miller Company was to American furniture design, Arteluce was to Italian lighting. Arteluce's owner, Gino Sarfatti, hired the best and brightest Italian designers to create innovative Modern lighting for his firm. Sarfatti founded the company in Milan in 1939, and designed all of its early products. A large percentage of Italy's post-World War II architecture included Arteluce lighting. Sarfatti won the first lighting awards ever given in Italy, the *Compasso d'Oro* in 1954 and again in 1955.

Gino Sarfatti was involved in his company at every level, from design to delivery. He experimented constantly with both design and lighting technology. His enthusiasm and energy attracted many young Italian designers of the time. Marco Zanuso, Franco Albini and Livio Castiglioni all produced cutting-edge lighting while associated with Sarfatti. By the mid 1950s Arteluce was internationally known.

In 1974 Sarfatti sold the company to his competitor, Flos. Arteluce remains an independent line within the larger company and still produces a number of Sarfatti's original designs. Arteluce stays true to the vision of its founder and continues to encourage the best young designers to apply their talent and ideas to the realm of lighting. Arteluce also produced a limited amount of furniture, but its furniture line was overshadowed by the tremendous success of its lamps.

The secondary market for good examples of Modern lighting is strong especially for Arteluce designs. There is often fierce competition at auctions when rare Arteluce pieces show up. New designs by Arteluce are expensive, so collectors can often pick up good examples for relatively reasonable prices on the secondary market.

FLOOR LAMP, c. 1950
Arteluce floor lamps tend to bring more money in the marketplace when their shades are multicolored.
$1,500–$2,000

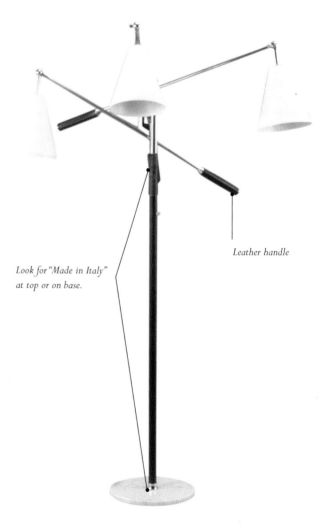

Leather handle

Look for "Made in Italy" at top or on base.

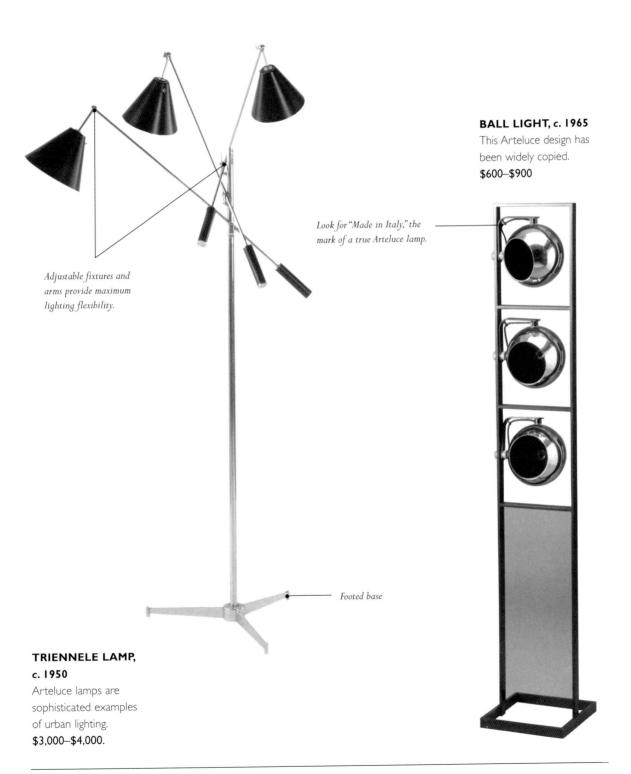

BALL LIGHT, c. 1965
This Arteluce design has been widely copied.
$600–$900

Look for "Made in Italy," the mark of a true Arteluce lamp.

Adjustable fixtures and arms provide maximum lighting flexibility.

Footed base

TRIENNELE LAMP, c. 1950
Arteluce lamps are sophisticated examples of urban lighting.
$3,000–$4,000.

Poul Henningsen Lamps

Who would have imagined that the PH series of lamps would remain fresh and current more than 75 years they were first designed. Poul Henningsen's prize-winning forms are not only still available but also still in great demand.

Henningsen was a Danish architect, born in 1894. Only four years after he started his architecture career he gained international acclaim after winning a competition for lighting the Danish Pavillion at the Paris World's Fair in 1924. This event marked the beginning of the PH series of lamps, which put Louis Poulsen & Company into production the same year. The first production model had a glass three-tiered shade that provided both direct and diffused light and masked the bulb from view. The fixture was simple and beautiful—a perfect example of functional Scandinavian design.

Henningsen believed along with many of his Danish contemporary designers that the best designs were those that were useful, well constructed and reasonably priced. His work met all three criteria.

Most of Henningsen's lighting revolves around a central theme of multiple layers or tiers of metal louvers. His most coveted design is the striking Artichoke Lamps, which was available in three sizes. It was first produced in 1957 and has been installed in numerous prestigious locations throughout the world.

The PH5, which also went into production in 1957, was Poul Henningsen's solution to a problem many lighting designers had failed to solve. This ingenious lamp provides good, strong light with no glare. This technology was not surpassed until the advent of the halogen fixture.

Henningsen's lighting proved so successful that it has often been reproduced, but never to the exacting standards of Louis Poulsen & Company.

The secondary market for Henningsen's work is strong but held in check by the fact that many of his designs are still being produced.

ARTICHOKE LAMP, c. 1960

An icon of 20th-century lighting design, Poul Henningsen's Artichoke hanging lamp features a brushed-copper exterior and a white enameled interior, a bright chrome lighting fixture, a hanging cord and ceiling plate.
$3,000–$4,000

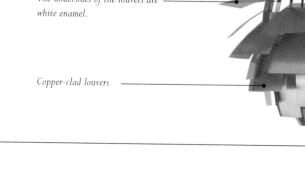

The actual lighting fixture is bright chrome.

The undersides of the louvers are white enamel.

Copper-clad louvers

MODERN EUROPEAN LIGHTING DESIGNS

KARL TRABERT
TABLE LAMP,
c. 1933

A black painted metal
and steel adjustable
table lamp, designed
by Karl Trabert for
G. Schanzebach.
$1,500–$2,250

POUL HENNINGSEN
TABLE LAMP, 1927

An early PH table lamp
designed by Poul
Henningsen in 1927
for Louis Poulsen
& Company.
$7,500–$10,500

DESNEY TABLE LAMP,
1935

A chromed metal and
glass table lamp,
manufactured by Desney.
$3,000–$4,500

CHRISTIAN DELL
SUPER DESK LAMP,
c. 1933

Model number 6580
Super desk lamp,
designed by Christian
Dell and manufactured
by Kaiser and Co.
$2,000–$3,000

Isamu Noguchi Lamps

Isamu Noguchi's vision of Modernism combines the best of Eastern and Western ideals, traditional and contemporary forms and natural and man-made materials to create objects that have withstood the test of time. His lighting designs provide a perfect example of this synthesis.

Trained as a sculptor, Noguchi turned to interior design in the late 1930s. Beginning in the 1940s, Herman Miller and Knoll produced several of his furniture designs. At the same time, Noguchi was experimenting with the idea of combining sculpture and light into luminous objects he called Lunars. These began to evolve into home lighting and eventually into the famous and much copied three-legged cylinder lamp produced by Knoll through the mid-1950s. Noguchi experimented with fiberglass and plastic shades, but the best-known of his lighting designs is the Japanese-inspired line of Akari paper lamps.

Whether the inspiration came from memories of his childhood in Japan or from a return trip he made there in 1951, it was the traditional, collapsible, candle-lit lanterns of Japan that motivated Noguchi to take his Lunars in a new direction. After returning to the United States, he began to design dozens of shades made from Japanese mulberry-bark paper and combined them with the most up-to-date lighting technology. The result, which Noguchi called Akari, Japanese for light, was a perfect confluence of 50s form, Japanese simplicity and American innovation. Produced in Japan, the Akari lamps mirror the abstract organic style of Noguchi's sculptures on a smaller scale. Although mass-produced, they are luminous sculpture, part art and part lighting.

The first Akari designs were more traditional. As Noguchi experimented with color, shape and proportion, the lamps grew bolder and more innovative. That they are still in production is a testament to Noguchi's lasting genius.

SMALL NOGUCHI LAMPS, c. 1970
Delicate and beautiful, Noguchi's lamps reflect a serene Japanese aesthetic.
$300–$500 each

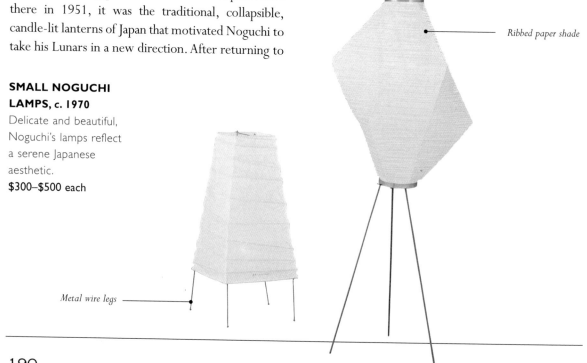

Ribbed paper shade

Metal wire legs

**TALL NOGUCHI
LAMPS, c. 1970**
Noguchi lamps come in a
variety of sizes and
shapes. Signed examples
are more valuable.
$500–$1,500 each

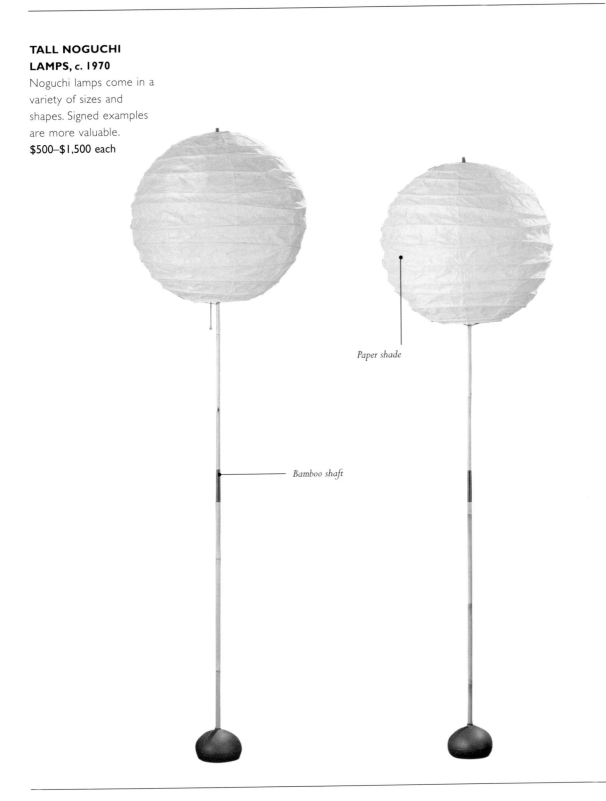

Paper shade

Bamboo shaft

Walter von Nessen Lamps

Walter von Nessen was born in 1889 in Germany where he trained as a metalworker. He immigrated to the United States in 1923 during a time of extraordinary prosperity and rapid innovation in industrial design. Although he designed furniture and decorative accessories, his lighting has proven to be his most lasting and important legacy.

Von Nessen opened a studio in New York City in 1927 and showed his famous swing-arm lamp that same year. By 1930, at the onset of the Depression, when many businesses were floundering, von Nessen's lighting catalog included more than 30 styles, which were much sought after by interior designers, architects and retail stores.

Throughout the 1930s, he also did work for other American companies including the Heisey Glass Company. His best-known association was with Chase Brass and Copper, which produced a number of his designs for lamps, bookends and other accessories and an award-winning coffee service.

Von Nessen's lamps represent a highly creative fusion of form, function and constantly evolving lighting technology. Flexible and functional, von Nessen's trendsetting lamps could bend and move, and tip, tilt and rotate in various directions. The light they produced was designed for specific purposes. Always incorporating the latest materials and technology, von Nessen's lighting designs remained fresh and progressive throughout his career. Both Eliel Saarinen and Florence Knoll favored his designs in their residential and commercial interiors.

His most notable lamps are the swing-arm lamp; his aluminum, glass and Bakelite table lamp produced in 1930; and the Lighthouse lamp which has two sections that can be turned on together or individually.

Von Nessen died in 1943. After World War II, his wife, Greta, revived the Nessen Studio, producing her husband's earlier designs and introducing new ones by herself and other designers. The company was sold in the early 1950s and again in the 1980s, when it was acquired by the Luxo Company, which still manufactures a number of von Nessen's enduring lighting designs.

VON NESSEN STYLE FLOOR LAMP, c. 1950

As a testament to their continuing appeal, many of von Nessen's lamps are still in production today.
$400–$600

Light fixture can swing into multiple positions.

Lamp shaft offset at base

POSTMODERNISM

Like many of the design movements of the 20th century, Postmodernism has sought a break with the past and conducted a fundamental reexamination of the relationship between form and function. Bold, brash, experimental and very often over-the-top, Postmodernism has been criticized for its lack of integrity, but like all successful design movements, it simply mirrors the values of society at large.

Late 20th-century Postmodernist design was a global reaction to the purist values of traditional Modernism. In Italy, Ettore Sottsass and the Memphis group brought together designers from around the world to collaborate on a new international style. Among them were the Americans Peter Shire and Michael Graves, the Japanese Shiro Kuramata and Arata Isozaki, the Italian Michele de Lucchi and the Englishman George Sowden. The Memphis group designed and produced furniture, lighting and ceramics that pushed the envelope of Modern design. Angular, playful and wildly colorful, the Memphis aesthetic challenged all prevailing notions of conventional design.

The Postmodern designers exploited new materials and technologies to create often startling sculptural furniture. Shiro Kuramata made his iconic How High the Moon chair out of expanded steel mesh. Frank Gehry used thick corrugated cardboard to fashion his Easy Edges furniture line, while Gaetano Pesce created his I Feltri chairs out of felt soaked in epoxy. Ron Arad, an Israeli working in London, has incorporated everything from found objects to aerospace materials and technologies in his cutting-edge furniture designs. The Postmodern pantheon also includes Australia's Marc Newson and France's Philippe Starck, both of whom have had a significant impact on the look of turn-of-the-21st-century furniture and interior design.

The last decades of the 20th century also witnessed a strong revival of the handcrafted studio furniture tradition. Building on the creative legacy of Wharton Esherick and George Nakashima, master craftsmen such as Albert Palley and Wendell Castle have used Postmodern influences to propel the studio furniture movement into the 21st century.

Ron Arad

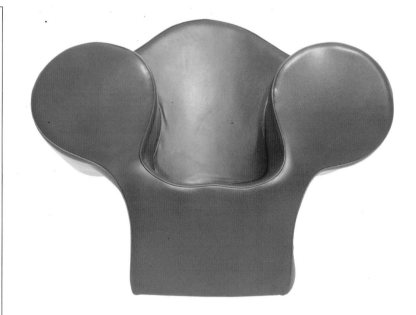

BIG EASY CHAIR, 1989
This witty easy chair is one of Arad's signature pieces.
$10,000–$20,000

ROVER CHAIR, c. 1981
Arad's use of nontraditional materials is evident in his Rover chair, which is constructed largely of found parts.
$5,000–$7,000

SINGLE RIETVELD CHAIR, 1991

Arad's dramatic homage to Gerrit Rietveld was produced in very limited numbers by his early design studio, One Off Ltd.
$20,000–$25,000

TOM VAC CHAIR, 1997

Produced by Vitra, the Tom Vac chair of molded polypropylene with steel or chrome legs is comfortable, stackable and fits equally well in home, office or on the patio.
$1,200–$1,500

STEEL LIGHT TABLE, 1988

Another rare Arad design from One Off Ltd.
$12,000–$18,000

Marc Newson

BUCKY CHAIR, 1995
An instant Postmodern "classic," the original plastic Bucky chairs were produced in very limited quantities and are now extremely rare.
$3,000–$4,000

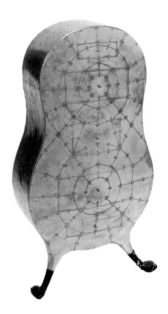

POD OF DRAWERS CABINET, 1987
Newson's second hand-beaten aluminum on fiberglass piece, the Pod of Drawers cabinet is even rarer than the Lockheed lounge, below. Recent auction estimates for one of the two existing examples range from $60,000 to $90,000.

LOCKHEED LOUNGE, 1986
Newson's breakthrough piece was the aluminum-on-fiberglass Lockheed lounge, a fluid metallic reinterpretation of an 18th-century chaise longue. Only 10 were made, and when one comes on the market, it can bring upwards of $100,000.

EVENT HORIZON TABLE, 1992
Newson's "funkily futuristic" aesthetic informs his sleek aluminum Event Horizon table.
$65,000–$80,000

COAST DINING CHAIRS, 1992
Among his many restaurant and hotel commissions, Newson designed these rectangular-back dining chairs for the now renamed London restaurant Coast.
$8,000–$10,000 the set of six

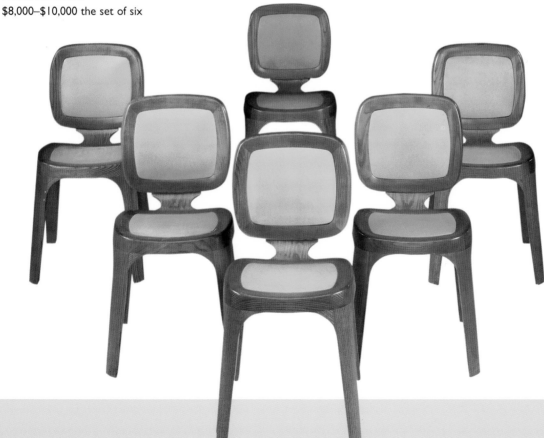

Ettore Sottsass

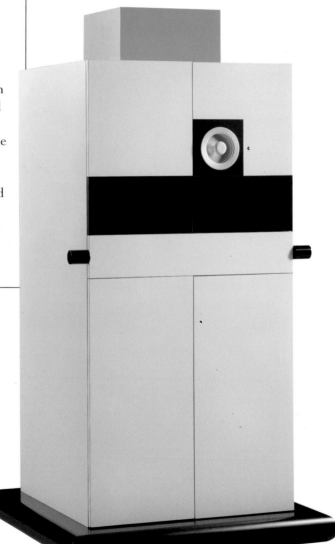

NIRVANA CABINET, 1966
Made of plastic laminate, wood and metal, the Nirvana cabinet is a restrained forerunner of ideas Sottsass would later elaborate on in his Memphis pieces.
$6,000–$9,000

CASABLANCA SIDEBOARD, 1981

One of Sottsass's most singular forms, the Casablanca sideboard is emblematic of the Postmodern Memphis style.
$8,000–$12,000

EASTSIDE LOUNGE, 1983

Produced by Knoll International, the Eastside sofas and chairs combined sleek, sophisticated lines with an offbeat interplay of colors.
$2,000–$3,000

Memphis

Founded by Ettore Sottsass, Memphis was a loose association of international designers and architects whose collective work quickly became emblematic of the "New Design" of the 1980s. (The name was inspired by Bob Dylan's song "Memphis Blues.") The group's first show opened in Milan on September 18, 1981, and brought together designers from Italy, France, Britain, Austria, Japan and the United States. It was a huge success.

Memphis designs caught the public's imagination with their bold colors, offbeat forms, and plastic-laminate surfaces. Playful, irreverent and liberating, the Memphis look was easy to imitate badly. The group disbanded in 1988. In addition to Sottsass, Memphis alumni include Mario Bellini, Michele de Lucchi, Michael Graves and Arata Isozaki.

DE LUCCHI KRISTAL TABLE, *c. 1981*

Looking more like a Postmodern pet than a functional piece of furniture, the de Lucchi Kristal table is a good example of the color sense and unfettered imagination that characterized the Memphis group. **$800–$1,200**

DE LUCCHI FIRST CHAIR, 1983

De Lucchi's metal-and-lacquered-wood First chair is a compelling design, but it's also surprisingly comfortable. **$400–$600 each**

SOTTSASS CARLTON
BOOKCASE, 1981

At once functional and playful, Sottsass's Carlton bookcase/room divider is one of the most impressive and monumental pieces to come out of the Memphis movement.

$12,000–$18,000

Wendell Castle

EARLY STOOL, c. 1965

When contrasted with the later pieces on these pages, this early Esherick-influenced stool underscores how far Castle's work has evolved and kept pace with current trends over the course of an illustrious 30-year-plus career.
$6,000–$9,000

INSIDER'S INFORMATION

Perhaps in response to the excesses of Postmodernism and Pop-culture plastic, the contemporary studio furniture movement underwent a renaissance during the last decades of the 20th century, and the undisputed leader of the movement has been Wendell Castle. Master sculptor, woodworker and furniture-maker, Castle has been instrumental in elevating handcrafted furniture into a respected and much sought after art form. His more recent work places him at the very cutting edge of furniture design.

CALIGARI READING STAND, c. 1989

Castle's reading stand is a dramatic example of Modern style applied to an ancient form.
$8,000–$12,000

BRIDGE BUFFET, 1994
In this outrageously organic piece, a three-drawer, scalloped mahogany case is mounted on a three-legged base sheathed in riveted and textured sheet copper.
$12,000–$15,000

CD HOLDER, 1991
Castle applies Modern style to a decidedly modern form in this unusual and whimsical limed-wood CD holder, anchored to a painted-steel "carpet."
$4,000–$6,000

Michael Graves

PIAZZA COFFEE AND TEA
SERVICE, 1980

Made of Bakelite, lacquered
aluminum, and mock ivory, this
extravagant set was designed by
Graves in 1980 and manufactured
by Alessi in 2000.
$20,000–$30,000

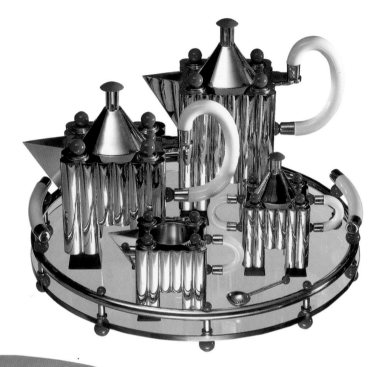

TABLE, c. 1989

Graves's architectural background is
clearly evident in the clean, elegant
lines of this table, produced for a
private commission.
$800–$1,200

INSIDER'S INFORMATION

One of the best-known and most prolific alumni of the Memphis group, Indianapolis-born Michael Graves is ranked among the world's foremost architects, but it is his product designs for everything from tea kettles to T-shirts that have made him a household name. Graves has made several important forays into furniture design, blending classical allusions with his trademark sense of whimsy.

PLAZA DRESSING TABLE AND STOOL, 1981

Graves created this over-the-top skyscraper take on the traditional vanity for the inaugural Memphis collection in 1981. These first Memphis designs were, for the most part, prototypes that were neither mass-produced nor stocked.

Gaetano Pesce

UP 5 LOUNGE CHAIR, c. 1969

Unconventional in form and packaging, Pesce's UP chairs were molded out of polyurethane foam, compressed under a vacuum and then wrapped in an airtight envelope. When opened and exposed to air, the chair would gradually regain its form and size.
$3,000–$4,000

SANSONE TABLE, c. 1985

A radical and dramatic Postmodern design for the adventurous collector.
$4,000–$6,000

I FELTRI CHAIRS, c. 1987

Pesce's I Feltri chairs are available
in high or low armchair versions.
Their frames are made of wool
felt impregnated with epoxy.
Low armchair $3,000–$4,000
High armchair $4,000–$5,000

SIT DOWN CHAIRS, c.1975

Inspired by the Pop sculpture of
Claes Oldenburg, Pesce's Sit Down
chairs were made of polyurethane
foam poured into quilted fabric.
$1,000–$2,000

Philippe Starck

INSIDER'S INFORMATION

Philippe Starck is perhaps best-known as one of today's leading designers of hotel, restaurant and nightclub interiors, but his unique Postmodern sensibility has informed a huge variety of objects, from noodles to door knobs, toothpick holders to lemon squeezers.

CHAIR AND TABLE GROUPING, c. 1990

Shown at left are two Teletables, designed for the Paramount Hotel in New York City in 1990; a pair of leather armchairs manufactured by Molinari; and two three-legged wood chairs (the rear leg is aluminum), designed for New York's Royalton Hotel. The chairs were never mass-produced.
Teletables $1,500–$2,000 the pair
Armchairs $2,500–$3,000 the pair
Chairs $400–$500 each

CAFÉ COSTES CHAIRS, c. 1982

Starck designed these sleek three-legged chairs for the Café Costes in Paris. Their value is enhanced when they are available in groups of more than four.
$300–$500 each

WHERE TO BUY AND SELL MODERN FURNITURE

Auction Houses

These auctioneers currently hold regular sales featuring Modern design. The list, however, is by no means exhaustive. As Modern design gains in popularity, more regional auction houses will begin adding Modern furniture sales to their yearly roster. A growing number of auctioneers, including all the major houses and many smaller ones, are posting their catalogues online. For more information on buying and selling 20th-century furniture at auction, see "Buying and Selling at Auction," pages 9–11.

USA

Christie's
20 Rockefeller Plaza,
New York, NY 10020
Tel: 212-636-2000
www.christies.com

L.A. Modern Auctions
PO Box 462006,
Los Angeles, CA 90046
Tel: 323-904-1950
www.lamodern.com

**Phillips, de Pury
& Luxembourg**
3 West 57th Street
New York, NY 10019
Tel: 212-940-1270
www.phillips-auctions.com

David Rago Auctions
333 North Main Street
Lambertville, NJ 08530
Tel: 609-397-9374
www.ragoarts.com

Sotheby's
1334 York Avenue
at 72nd Street
New York, NY 10021
Tel: 212-606-7000
www.sothebys.com

Wright20
1140 W. Fulton
Chicago, IL 60607
Tel: 312-563-0020
www.wright20.com

EUROPE

Bonhams
101 New Bond Street,
London, UK
Tel: +44-20-7629-6602
www.bonhams.com

Christie's
85 Old Brompton Road
London, UK
Tel: +44-20-7581-7611
www.christies.com

**Hagelstam Fine Art
Auctioneers**
Bulevardi 9 A,
00120 Helsinki
FINLAND
Tel: +358-9-602-785
www.hagelstam.com

**Phillips, de Pury
& Luxembourg**
49 Grosvenor Street
London, UK
Tel: +44-20-7318-4010
www.phillips-auctions.com

Sotheby's
34-35 New Bond Street
London, UK
Tel: +44-20-7493-8080
www.sothebys.com

Dealers

The ranks of dealers specializing in 20th-century furniture has grown tremendously in recent years. Following is a far from comprehensive sampling.

USA

Henrik Aarestrup
147 Main Street
Sharon, CT 06069
Tel: 860-364-7071

John Alexander Ltd.
10–12 West Gravers Lane
Philadelphia PA 19118
Tel: 215-242-0741
www.johnalexanderltd.com

Antik
104 Franklin Street
New York, NY 10013
Tel: 212-343-0471
www.antik-nyc.net

Maurice Bean Studios
4125 Crutchfield Street
Richmond, VA 23225
Tel: 804-233-6257

**Nicholas and Shaunna
Brown**
P.O. Box 1044
Camden, ME 04843
Tel/Fax: 207-236-8492
NickandShaunna@earthlink.net

Calderwood Gallery
1427 Walnut Street
Philadelphia, PA 19102
Tel: 215-568-7475
www.calderwoodgallery.com

Collage 20th Century Classics
2820 North Henderson Avenue
Dallas, TX 75206
Tel: 214-828-9888
Fax: 214-828-9888
www.collageclassics.com

Galerie de Beyrie
393 West Broadway
New York, NY 10012
Tel: 212-219-9565
Fax: 212-965-1348
www.galeriedebeyrie.com

TWENTIETH-CENTURY DESIGNERS: A QUICK REFERENCE GUIDE

This easy-access guide provides capsule descriptions of the work and influence of the designers and producers of Modern furniture featured in this book. The Quick Reference Guide is also a handy navigating tool, listing all primary references in the book to each featured designer or company.

Aalto, Alvar (1898–1976) Trained as an architect in his native Finland, Aalto designed furniture, lighting, glass and textiles that was practical, simple and beautifully made. The quality and moderate price of his work made it very popular in postwar America.　**pages 64, 126**

Arad, Ron (1951–) Israeli-born, London-based Arad is an emblematic figure of the Postmodern furniture movement. Dramatic designs in non-traditional materials are hallmarks of his work.　**page 194**

Archizoom Associati This late 1960s design collective produced cutting-edge furniture infused with a Pop-kitsch sensibility.　**page 86**

Arteluce From its founding in 1939 by Gino Sarfatti, Arteluce has attracted the best and brightest Italian designers to create innovative Modern lighting.　**page 186**

Bertoia, Harry (1915–1978) Born in Italy, Bertoia produced some of 20th-century America's most distinctive industrial and artistic forms, including jewelry, sculpture and iconic furniture designs, such as the Bird chair and the Diamond chair.　**page 46**

Brandt, Edgar (1860–1960) The master of French Art Deco metalwork, Brandt produced exquisite lighting designs, often with shades by the Daum glassworks of Nancy, France.　**pages 31, 60, 177**

Breuer, Marcel (1902–1981) One of the giants of the Modern movement, Breuer pioneered the use of tubular metal in furniture construction and had a tremendous impact on 20th-century furniture design.　**pages 56, 131**

Castle, Wendell (1932–) Master sculptor, woodworker and furniture-maker, Castle is the undisputed leader of the contemporary studio furniture movement and has played a key role in elevating handcrafted furniture into a respected and much sought after art form.　**pages 128, 202**

Cheuret, Albert (1884–1966) Cheuret's lighting designs typify the elegance and exuberance of French Art Deco. **pages 61, 176**

Deskey, Donald (1894–1989) The designer of the interior of New York's Radio City Music Hall also provided high-styled furniture that defined the standard for American Deco.　**page 100**

Eames, Charles (1907–1978) **and Ray** (1912–1988) Arguably the greatest husband-and-wife design team of the 20th century, perhaps of all time, the Eameses had a tremendous impact on interior environments—both domestic and commercial—the world over. Their influence encompasses architecture, furniture, graphics, textiles, photography, film and even toys.　**pages 146, 148, 150, 156, 158**

Esherick, Wharton (1887–1970) The artistry of Wharton Esherick, fully exemplified in the interior design of his Pennsylvania house and studio, bridged the gap between rural arts and crafts and sophisticated urban design.　**page 138, 184**

Evans, Paul (d. 1987) One of the most prolific and versatile artists of the mid-century studio furniture movement, Evans incorporated revolutionary combinations of materials in his boldly dramatic and sculptural furniture designs.　**pages 122, 164, 184**

Fornasetti, Piero (1913–1998) Bucking the predominant trend of 20th-century Modernism, Fornasetti celebrated ornamentation and used his trompe-l'oeil technique to chide the prevailing art establishment.　**page 144**

Frankl, Paul (1886–1962) America's love affair with the skyscraper was a source of inspiration for Frankl. His Skyscraper cabinets are considered to be the first wholly original American furniture design.　**page 110**

Gehry, Frank O. (1929–) Like his award-winning architecture, Gehry's furniture designs are startling and innovative. He uses inexpensive materials, such as corrugated cardboard, in new ways, rendering them into highly original sculptural forms. **page 90**

Girard, Alexander (1907–1993) Known primarily for his eye-catching textile designs for the Herman Miller Company, Girard also designed graphics, restaurant interiors and a sleek, sophisticated line of furniture derived from a commission for Braniff International Airways. **page 80**

Graves, Michael (1934–) One of the world's foremost architects, Graves is also one of the best-known and most prolific alumni of the Memphis Group. His product designs for everything from tea kettles to T-shirts have made him a household name. **page 204**

Henningsen, Poul (1894–1967) Danish architect Poul Henningsen's lighting designs have remained fresh and current more than 75 years after they were first designed. His 1960 Artichoke lamp has become an icon of 20th-century lighting design. **page 188**

The Herman Miller Company The furniture produced by the Herman Miller Company of Zeeland, Michigan, defines innovation in American Modern design. The company's relationships with such mid-century masters as Gilbert Rohde, George Nelson, Charles and Ray Eames, Isamu Noguchi and Alexander Girard made it a leader in progressive-furniture production. **pages 145–160**

Heywood-Wakefield A mainstay of mid-century Modern design, Heywood-Wakefield furniture was purchased by thousands of American families during the postwar boom and is widely available and sought after in today's market. **pages 102, 161**

Hoffman, Josef (1870–1956) As a founding member of the Vienna Secession movement and the Wiener Werkstätte, Hoffman was a pivotal figure in the early development of 20th-century Modernism. **page 54**

Iosa Ghini, Massimo (1959–) Inspired by the biomorphic forms of the 1950s and futuristic space-age designs, Iosa Ghini's furniture is claiming its place in the Modern canon for its innovation, bold lines and quality craftsmanship. **page 88**

Jacobsen, Arne (1902–1971) Throughout the 1950s and 60s, Jacobsen helped bring Danish design into international prominence, moving it away from its handcrafted wood beginnings to a sleek new industrial aesthetic. His Egg, Swan and Ant chairs have become an indispensable part of the 20th century's design vocabulary. **page 84**

Juhl, Finn (1912–1989) One of the most influential Danish Modern designers, Juhl created furniture that combines the best in Danish craftsmanship with Modern organic design. Collectors should beware of copies as Juhl's work was widely imitated. **page 76**

Kagan, Vladimir (1927–) Although his name is synonymous with an organic, curvilinear style of furniture, Kagan worked in a wide range of styles, from Bauhaus geometric to his 1960s experiments with new materials and minimalist forms. **pages 72, 170**

Knoll, Florence (1917–) In collaboration with her husband, Hans, Florence Knoll created furniture and interior designs that still influence the way modern corporate offices look and function. The hallmarks of Knoll furniture are spare lines, boxy design and high-quality construction. **pages 44, 134**

Le Corbusier (1887–1965) A 20th-century design visionary, Le Corbusier championed the use of industrial materials and standardized functional furniture. His influence on 20th-century architecture, urban-planning and design was enormous. His furniture designs, however, were often collaborative efforts, making attribution difficult. **page 62**

Loewy, Raymond (1893–1986) One of the most prolific industrial designers of the 20th century, Loewy was a pioneer of 1930s Streamline style and designed everything from the iconic Coke bottle to the interior of the NASA Skylab. His 1960s acrylic furniture is highly collectible. **page 168**

Mackintosh, Charles Rennie (1868–1928) Glasgow-born Mackintosh was one of the most significant architects/designers working at the turn of the 20th century. His furniture designs drew on Art Nouveau, Scottish and Japanese influences, and original pieces are among the costliest in today's market. **page 50**

McArthur, Warren (1885–1961) McArthur's innovative tubular metal furniture was hugely popular in 1930s Hollywood and is much sought after today. **page 106**

McCobb, Paul (1907–1978) In the 1950s McCobb's well built, well designed and affordably priced furniture for Directional Furniture Company helped bring quality Modern design into the average American home. Produced in large quantities, McCobb pieces remain affordable on the secondary market. **page 136**

Mies van der Rohe, Ludwig (1886-1969) A master of Modern design and a pioneer in the use of tubular metal in Modern furniture, Mies is best known for his signature Barcelona chair. **page 58**

Memphis Group Founded by Ettore Sottsass in 1981, Memphis was a loose association of international designers and architects whose work shook the world of furniture and object design with its bold colors, offbeat forms and plastic-laminate surfaces. **page 200**

Nakashima, George (1905–1990) His work exemplifies the best of mid-century studio furniture. Throughout his career, Nakashima explored the organic expressiveness of wood, often choosing boards with knots and figured grain for his signature studio pieces. He also designed production lines for Knoll and Widdicomb. **pages 82, 116, 140, 184**

Nelson, George (1907–1986) Best known for such Modern design icons as the Marshmallow sofa, the Atomic clock, and the Bubble lamp, Nelson also reinvigorated the concept of personal storage through his highly successful storage lines. **pages 152, 154, 160, 162, 180, 182**

Newson, Marc (1962–) Australian-born, London-based Newson creates "funkily futuristic" aerodynamic furniture that is bringing high prices on the secondary market. His plastic Bucky chair and aluminum-on-fiberglass Lockheed lounge were instant Postmodern "classics." **page 196**

Noguchi, Isamu (1904–1988) In his sculpture, as well as in his groundbreaking biomorphic furniture and Japanese-inspired lighting designs, Noguchi synthesized Eastern and Western design ideals, natural and man-made materials and traditional and contemporary forms. **pages 118, 190**

Pesce, Gaetano (1939–) One of the more radical and idiosyncratic of the postwar Italian designers, Pesce has experimented widely and successfully with new forms and materials such as the epoxy-impregnated wool of his I Feltri chairs. **page 206**

Ponti, Gio (1891–1979) Ponti's elegant furniture pays homage to classical forms while looking ahead to the next innovation in technology and design. His designs encompassed everything from buildings and furniture to glass, ceramics, textiles and appliances. **page 124**

Powell, Phillip Lloyd In his New Hope, PA, studio, Phil Powell produced seating and storage pieces characterized by impeccable craftsmanship, flowing lines and deeply carved details. More than other studio designers, Powell personalized his work, incorporating references to his life and artistic journey. **pages 70, 166, 184**

Prouvé, Jean (1901–1984) Designed primarily for offices, schools and hospitals, Prouvé's functional, minimalist furniture is a unique example of machine-based craftsmanship that bridged the gap between art and industry. Highly original, even revolutionary, Prouvé's work commands high prices at auction. **page 132**

Rietveld, Gerrit (1888–1964) This influential Dutch architect/designer sought to reduce furniture pieces to their most elemental planes and to design avant-garde furniture that could be sold at department-store prices. His breakthrough design was the Mondrianesque Red-Blue chair of 1918. **page 52**

Robsjohn-Gibbings, Terence Harold (1905–1976) English-born designer Robsjohn-Gibbings created an impressive portfolio of furniture designs for Widdicomb, all in a conservative yet stylish Modern idiom. A lifelong admirer of classical Greek forms, he designed a Greek-inspired line of furniture late in his career. **pages 113, 142**

Rohde, Gilbert (1894–1944) An important bridge between European Art Deco and American Modern, Rohde's furniture, such as the Paldao Group and his chrome pieces, are highly prized by collectors. His early Modern clocks for the Herman Miller Clock Company also command premium prices. **pages 98, 112, 174**

Saarinen, Eero (1910–1961) Like his famous father, Eliel, Eero Saarinen made his mark in architecture and furniture design. His 1957 Tulip Pedestal Group of chairs, tables and stools went on to become an emblematic 1960s design, bringing Saarinen's brand of architectural Modernism into interiors across America. **page 114**

Saarinen, Eliel (1873–1950) The great Finnish architect had a major impact on 20th-century American design through his own work and through his groundbreaking program at the Cranbrook Academy of Art in Michigan, where he mentored some of the leading postwar designers, including his son, Eero. **page 104**

Schoen, Eugene (1880–1957) The epitome of the grace and sophistication of American Deco design, Schoen's furniture is much admired today for its warmth, refined elegance and subtle use of color. **page 108**

Schultz, Richard (1926–) Schultz is best known for his 1960 Petal tables, produced by Knoll to accompany Bertoia chairs, and his Leisure Group of outdoor furniture. The 1990s Café Collection is bringing Schultz' vision to a new generation of homeowners. **page 120**

Sottsass, Ettore (1917–) A prime mover of Italian design since 1947, Sottsass has brought his creativity to bear on the fields of architecture, furniture design, ceramics, and graphics. A founding member of Memphis, he designed some of its most distinctive furniture pieces. **page 198, 200**

Starck, Philippe (1949–) Best known as a leading designer of hotel, restaurant and nightclub interiors, Starck has designed everything from furniture to noodles in his unique Postmodern idiom. **page 208**

Stendig, Charles A creative marketer with an eye for art, Stendig introduced a shocked and delighted American public to cutting-edge Italian design of the 1960s. Among the signature pieces imported by Stendig are the Marilyn Love Seat and the Cactus coatrack. **page 78**

Von Nessen, Walter (1889–1943) Trained as a metalworker in his native Germany, von Nessen introduced his famous swing-arm lamp in his New York studio in 1927. Although he designed furniture and decorative accessories, von Nessen's lighting designs are his most important legacy. **page 192**

Wegner, Hans (1914–) In the work of Danish designer and master cabinetmaker Hans Wegner, form and materials are equal partners. His furniture designs, such as the Bull chair and the famous Round chair, embody the quality, practicality and simplicity of Danish Modern. **page 74**

Wormley, Edward (1907–1995) In collaboration with the Dunbar Furniture Company, Wormley translated the hard-edged Modern vocabulary into highly successful lines of livable, conservative yet sophisticated furniture. **pages 65, 95**

Wright, Frank Lloyd (1867–1959) Arguably the most famous American architect, Wright designed most of his furniture as part of architectural commissions. A line he designed for Heritage-Henredon in the 1950s met with only limited success. **pages 68, 93**

INDEX

Page numbers in *italic* refer
to images.

BIBLIOGRAPHY

Bernsen, Jens. *Hans J. Wegner*, Copenhagen: Danish Design Center, 1995.

Byars, Mel. *The Design Encyclopedia*, London: Calmann & King, 1994.

Droste, Magdalena and Manfred, Ludewig. *Marcel Breuer*, Cologne: Benedikt Taschen Verlag, 1992.

Duncan, Alistair. *Art Deco Furniture: The French Designers*, London: Thames and Hudson, 1984.

Duncan, Alistair. *Modernism—Modernist Design 1880–1940*, Minneapolis: Norwest Corporation, 1998.

Eidelberg, Martin, ed. *Design 1935–1965: What Modern Was*, New York: Harry N. Abrams, 1991.

Fahr–Becker, Gabriele. *Wiener Werkstatte: 1903–1932*, Cologne: Benedikt Taschen Verlag, 1995.

Fiell, Charlotte and Peter. *Design of the Twentieth Century*, Cologne: Benedikt Taschen Verlag, 1999.

Fiell, Charlotte and Peter. *Fifties Decorative Art*, Cologne: Benedikt Taschen Verlag, 2000.

Fiell, Charlotte and Peter. *1,000 Chairs*, Cologne: Benedikt Taschen Verlag, 1997.

Fiell, Charlotte and Peter. *Sixties Decorative Art*, Cologne: Benedikt Taschen Verlag, 2000.

Fiell, Charlotte and Peter. *Seventies Decorative Art*, Cologne: Benedikt Taschen Verlag, 2000.

Hiesingerm, Kathryn B. and Marcus, George H. *Landmarks of Twentieth Century Design: An Illustrated Handbook*, New York: Abbeville Press, 1993.

Hiort, Esbjorn. *Finn Juhl*, Copenhagen: Danish Architectural Press, 1990.

Neuhart, John, Neuhart, Marilyn and Eames, Ray. *Eames Design: The Work of the Office of Charles and Ray Eames*, New York: Harry N. Abrams, 1989.

Neumann, Claudia. *Design Directory: Italy*, New York: Universe, 1999.

Oda, Noritsugu. *Danish Chairs*, Tokyo: Korinsha Press & Co., 1996.

Pina, Leslie. *Classic Herman Miller*, Atglen: Schiffer, 1998.

Pina, Leslie. *Fifties Furniture*, Atglen: Schiffer, 1996.

Polster, Bernd. *Design Directory: Scandinavia*, New York: Universe, 1999.

Rouland, Steven and Linda. *Knoll Furniture: 1938–1960*, Atglen, PA: Schiffer, 1999.

Sparke, Penny. *A Century of Design: Design Pioneers of the Twentieth Century*, London: Mitchell Beazley, 1998.

Stimpson, Miriam F. *Modern Furniture Classics*, London: Architectural Press, 1987.

The Long Chair by George Nakashima was designed and manufactured in 1958.

PICTURE CREDITS

All pictures supplied by **David Rago Auctions, Lambertville, New Jersey**, except the following:

Arad Associates, photo by William Moser: page 195 (middle);

Christie's Images: pages 52, 54, 55 (top), 62, 63, 109, 119 (bottom), 139 (bottom), 195 (bottom), 196 (middle and bottom), 197 and 205;

Courtesy of the Wharton Esherick Museum, photography by Mansfield Bascom, Curator: page 185 (left);

Angelo Hornak Library, courtesy of the V&A: page 61 (bottom);

Balthazar Korab Ltd.: page 104 (bottom);

L.A. Modern Auctions: pages 44, 49, 58 (bottom), 59 (top), 187 (left), 194 (bottom) and 207 (top);

Mitchell Beazley: page 159;

Phillips Fine Art Auctions: pages 53, 57 (top), 194 (top), 195 (top), 196 (top);

Richard Schultz: pages 120 and121;

Sotheby's Picture Library: pages 31 (top), 50, 51, 55 (bottom), 61 (top right and top left), 157 (top) and 177;

Treadway Gallery: pages 112 (top) and 208 (top);

Virginia Museum of Fine Art: page 101.